Marty & Gayle

UNLOCK THE
GROWTH
POTENTIAL
OF YOUR
ORGANIZATION

Carl

CARL F. HICKS, JR, PH.D
& MARTIN E. WILLOUGHBY, JR., J.D.

HighImpactPublishing
www.highimpactpublishing.com

High Impact Publishing
Chevy Chase, MD

ISBN: 1502519755
ISBN 13: 9781502519757
Library of Congress Control Number: 2014917377
CreateSpace Independent Publishing Platform
North Charleston, South Carolina

OTHER PUBLICATIONS BY THE AUTHORS

By Martin

Zoom Entrepreneur

By Carl

High Impact Ideas For Your Life

DEDICATION

To our clients, coaches, teachers and mentors.

TABLE OF CONTENTS

Foreword · ix
Chapter 1 Introduction · 1
Chapter 2 Why Be Your Best? · · · · · · · · · · · · · · · · · · 15
Chapter 3 How to Work With Me · · · · · · · · · · · · · · · · 25
Chapter 4 How To Talk To Me · · · · · · · · · · · · · · · · · 33
Chapter 5 Biggest Mistakes You Can Make With Me · · · · · · · · · 41
Chapter 6 How to Incentivize Me? · · · · · · · · · · · · · · · · 49
Chapter 7 Motivating Me For Best Performance · · · · · · · · · · · 57
Chapter 8 Why Should I Help Others Be Their Best? · · · · · · · · · 67
Chapter 9 How Do I Help Others Be Their Best? · · · · · · · · · · · 75
Chapter 10 Call to Action · 85

Appendix A How to Effectively Use the Results of the *UMMD*™
Report · 89

Appendix B Carl's *Understanding My Motivational Drivers*™ Report
Martin's *Understanding My Motivational Drivers*™
Report · 93

About the Authors · 109

Additional Resources Available
From The Growth Group, LLC ·111

"Leadership is unlocking people's potential to become better."

— BILL BRADLEY

FOREWORD

Organizations exist to accomplish feats that no single individual can do alone. The efficient and effective combination of resources—minds, money, material, methods and motives to achieve results--requires effective leaders. Leaders, who can find, attract, develop and retain talented people. Leaders, who can provide clarity of focus and direction that inspires others to strive for their personal best. Leaders, who understand and appreciate people's needs and expectations. Understanding the needs and expectations of people is the key to unlocking the growth potential of any organization.

How, then, does a person striving to be an effective leader readily grasp the needs of others? Unfortunately, people don't walk around with signs stating the best way to interact with them.

Effective leaders are usually effective coaches. They possess a high degree of self-awareness. They understand their own strengths and struggles. They know what they don't know and are dedicated to closing their personal knowledge gaps. They are not stagnant. They are growth oriented, willing to learn and able to change as conditions dictate.

A keen awareness of self and others is required to unlock the performance potential of each person in an organization. A leader's responsibility is to provide good stewardship of the organization's assets. Understanding the motivational drivers of others, while not always easy, is an essential trait of effective leaders. Each individual has needs, preferences and motivational drivers that are important to them. They know how they prefer to work; how they want people to talk with them and what incentivizes them.

Certain actions, words or initiatives by a leader may motivate a person to give their best or turn out to be a huge mistake. Effective leaders strive to understand the uniqueness of each individual. And, they tailor their leadership efforts to be in alignment with each person's uniqueness. Effective leaders learn to lead based on the motivational drivers of each individual. Effective leaders focus first on bringing out the best in others and then on helping others understand, embrace, pursue and achieve worthwhile objectives.

An effective leader is a self-aware leader. A self-aware leader recognizes that their leadership action can be viewed favorably by one person and unfavorably by another person. A self-aware leader strives constantly to be aware of his/her impact on the performance of another person.

The key to unlocking the growth potential of an organization is to understand the motivational drivers of each person in five critical areas. Namely,

- How they prefer to work
- How they want to be talked to
- Mistakes to avoid making with them
- How they want to be incentivized
- Creating conditions that motivate them for best performance

This book introduces a powerful self-awareness tool: the **Understanding My Motivational Drivers™ (UMMD™)** Report that could very well be the key that unlocks the potential of your organization. In Chapter 10 you'll find a coupon code that permits you to take the **UMMD™** self-assessment on line at a reduced price. This self-assessment provides the opportunity for you to review and confirm your own motivational drivers and offers you a vehicle with which to share and discuss your information with others. Imagine if everyone in your organization had access to this powerful tool. Imagine unlocking the untapped potential of your organization. Imagine the elevation of performance that could be realized.

The core chapters in this book describe the five essential elements of the *UMMD*™ Report.

In writing this book, we, the authors, utilized our respective *UMMD*™ Reports to exchange and discuss our needs and expectations of how we could each bring out the best in one another and by doing so unleash our potential. Let us know how well you think we did.

"When we seek to discover the best in others, we somehow bring out the best in ourselves."

—WILLIAM ARTHUR WARD (1921-1994)

CHAPTER 1:

INTRODUCTION

Unlocking Growth Potential

Organizations are full of growth potential: potent forces that can be, but have not yet, come into being. To be realized, this growth potential must be unlocked. Unleashed growth potential can be observed in an individual's outstanding performance. It can be found in the creativity and collaboration of teams. Other times we see it expressed in the excellence of customer service. We can also appreciate it in the functionality and beauty of a product's design. Both elevated performance and profitability are accepted indicators of an organization's growth potential transformed into results.

Underlying all of these positive organizational indicators, of course, are people. How can we help organizational participants unleash their growth potential? Is there a tool, method or process that can take the guesswork out of understanding others? Is there a key that can be used to unlock a person's growth potential? We think there is and it is being introduced and explained in this book.

The tool, ***Understanding My Motivational Drivers™ (UMMD™)*** is a self-assessment built on the chassis of the Birkman Method®--a multifaceted personality assessment that provides practical insights into everyday issues impacting our lives and work. The present format was conceived by Carl and has been extensively tested by both Carl and Martin in their respective coaching practices. Each of the five topics in the report contains statements driven by the person's responses to three online questionnaires.

The topics are:

- How to work with me
- How to talk with me
- Biggest mistakes you can make with me
- How to incentivize me
- Motivating me for best performance

It takes less than forty-five minutes to complete the three questionnaires that yield customized, personal, and valuable information about one's motivational drivers. But the journey to awareness doesn't stop there. Each participant is given the opportunity to review their motivational drivers and then confirm that the items listed are, in fact, significant to them. In short, they confirm their most important expectations of how they want to be treated by others.

But, there's more. The report recipient is then encouraged to share and discuss their most significant motivational drivers with a friend, team member, supervisor, colleague, professional associate, business partner, coach, team leader, employee, trusted advisor, client/customer, or peer. This opportunity to share and discuss personal needs and expectations with others can make a meaningful difference in a person's life.

That is what we are trying to do with this book — make a meaningful difference in your life. We want you to be the best *you* that you can be! Life is too short and time too precious to waste on being dissatisfied or unhappy because someone is not treating you in accordance with your expectations.

Take control of your life. Let others know your needs and expectations. Be accountable for your own happiness and success. Unleash your greatness!

Enhanced awareness of motivational drivers can improve our inter-action alignment with others. A closer alignment between one's behav-ior and another's motivational drivers will have a positive impact on the productivity and engagement level of both people. Bringing out the best in others is a win-win for all.

Within an organizational setting, bringing out the best in others can lead to more actively engaged employees. Actively engaged employees are typically more productive. More productive employees can have a positive impact on an organization's financial metrics.

We are passionate about sharing this relationship between leading others based on an enhanced understanding of their motivational drivers and the potential positive impacts on the organization. We are energized when others realize their potential.

Martin and Carl (Project Plan)

Before one word of this book was written we, Martin and Carl, decided to jointly review our respective *UMMD*™ Reports. While we've been collaborating for several years on a number of strategic thinking initia-tives, we'd never attempted a project as complex as writing a book.

The insight and increased awareness that resulted from sharing and discussing our motivational drivers was remarkable. While we were somewhat aware of the differences in our perspectives and approaches to work, we both came away from our discussion with a renewed appre-ciation for the most effective ways to approach this project.

Table 1.1
A Sample Comparison of Martin and Carl's
Motivational Drivers

TOPICS	MARTIN	CARL
HOW TO WORK WITH ME	Avoid imposing structured plans on me if at all possible	Be direct and straightforward with me
HOW TO TALK TO ME	Encourage me to think "outside the box" if you really want to engage my attention	Emphasize those results which will offer benefits to others as well as to me, or which will support my system of personal values
BIGGEST MISTAKES YOU CAN MAKE WITH ME	It's a mistake to measure my performance by watching how busy I am	It's a mistake to push me to make up my mind quickly
HOW TO INCENTIVIZE ME	Unorthodox incentives often work well with me	Reward only my attainment of demanding, meaningful achievements
MOTIVATING ME FOR BEST PERFORMANCE	I need to feel self-confident about tasks that I may take on if I'm to feel strongly motivated	I often respond well to ambitious targets and goals

Source: Understanding My Motivational Drivers™ Reports for Martin Willoughby and Carl Hicks

An Important Life Lesson

As a newly hired manager with ten employees, I (Carl) thought it best to get to know each person and their respective job responsibilities early on. Most of these employees had worked together for at least one year; some had been employed for ten years or more. At twenty-nine years of age, I was at least a decade younger that most of the team. I was the newcomer. By my second week on the job, I started making it a point to visit briefly with each person once a week to provide positive and specific feedback.

On Friday afternoons, I visited with Mrs. Orr, our budgeting and finance specialist. By my sixth week on the job, Mrs. Orr had prepared a thorough analysis that was successfully used to justify three new positions. The Vice President was impressed with the analysis and that day I had my usual appreciative dialog with her.

After sharing my thanks with Mrs. Orr, she asked me if I was still interested in hearing ideas about how to improve employee productivity. I assured her I was. She then informed me that she could improve her personal productivity by 20% if I'd eliminate my Friday dialogs with her. Aghast, I asked why. She informed me that she was a professional, knew when she had done a job or task well, and didn't need me to bring it to her attention. Unable to think of anything else to say I thanked her for her feedback and left her office.

Mrs. Orr's Perspective

Mrs. Orr, I later found out, had always been easily embarrassed by praise. She struggled with compliments paid to her. Her formative years involved a strict upbringing where the focus was on not making mistakes. She learned that lesson well and adopted a belief system that "no news was indeed good news." She simply didn't know how to handle my appreciative dialog process. Later I found out from another employee that the thought of my stopping by each Friday was stressful for Mrs. Orr. All day on Friday she'd be nervous and ill at ease. In essence, I was ruining her life!

Lesson Learned

Mrs. Orr taught me a valuable life lesson. My efforts to provide positive feedback and recognition were based more on *my* need for recognition than on *Mrs. Orr's* needs. I was trying to interact with Mrs. Orr using a method that worked for me. My leadership imperative was to bring out the best in Mrs. Orr while helping her to understand, embrace, pursue, and achieve worthwhile initiatives. I'd clearly failed in that regard. To this day, I grieve over my lack of awareness, and I'm deeply grateful to Mrs. Orr for caring enough to speak up.

Mrs. Orr helped me to become aware that I should have embraced what Dr. Tony Alessandra coined as the "Platinum Rule." Namely, "treat others the way they want to be treated." Once I absorbed this lesson, Mrs. Orr and I went on to enjoy a great working relationship that lasted another six years. Interacting with her based on *her* motivational drivers and not mine enabled her to utilize her unique abilities and flourish. She was happy, less stressed, and able to thrive as an actively engaged employee. In short, she was at her best, and the organization, her coworkers, and I were the beneficiaries of her performance.

Let's take a deeper look at my failed interaction with Mrs. Orr and analyze my missteps.

How to Work with Her

Mrs. Orr was self-directed. Her work, for the most part, was repetitive and revolved around the monthly accounting cycle. Although she was friendly and respectful, she preferred to work alone and with *things* (i.e. numbers) rather than people. She preferred a protected work environment free of interruptions (like my Friday visits). She perceived my weekly appreciative dialogs as an invasion of her work environment, while I thought my visit would be the highlight of her week.

How to Talk with Her

If a conversation between the two of us was required, she would initiate it. Usually, however, there was little need to do so as she knew her job very well. When responding to questions, she was thoughtful, accurate, and to the point. I, on the other hand, tended to explain too much of the "why" behind a request or question. Today, I can easily appreciate how my need to explain in some detail, in order to secure "buy in" from her, conflicted with her need to be brief and to the point. She readily accepted assignments without questioning them. She didn't need me to persuade or inspire her to do her job.

To summarize, I (Carl) failed to understand Mrs. Orr's motivational drivers. My awareness of her real needs was woefully inadequate. My perspective on how to effectively interact with her was out of focus and centered on my needs. By interacting with her based primarily on my perspective and my needs, I caused a very good employee (and person) unnecessary stress, diminished her engagement with her job, negatively impacted her enjoyment of her job, and caused her to be less productive.

I'm grateful to Mrs. Orr for this most valuable life lesson. She helped me see that even a well-meaning interaction from a manager can have a negative impact on an employee's attitude, level of engagement, and performance.

Examples of What We Have Observed in Our Business and Consulting Experience

- After reviewing the "How to incentivize me" section of his **UMMD™** Report, an executive of a health care firm wondered out loud (to Carl and Martin) if the decision to have one employee incentive program for all levels of employees might need to be reevaluated.

- A senior Sales Manager of a financial services organization expressed to Carl his frustration with his group of new, young recruits who didn't seem to be as motivated by money as he was. Upon closer examination, money was important to this group of Millennials, but not at the expense of their lifestyle. Was this a generational difference? A difference in perspective? A difference in importance of motivational drivers? Or, a combination of all three?

- A president of a successful company in the Southeast contacted Carl in search of an executive coach. When asked why he was seeking a coach, the president said that he needed someone to hold him accountable. Without crossing the line between being an effective consultant and an "insultant," Carl responded that only the president could hold himself accountable, to do otherwise would be avoiding personal accountability. The president hired Carl on the spot, explaining that this simple, obvious comment immediately changed his perspective. After six months of coaching, the president also stopped trying to hold other people accountable. That was their job not his.

- In a team-strengthening experience facilitated by Carl, two groups of senior managers from an international oil company were given the same assignment: clarify, compile, summarize, and prioritize a list of twenty-five items the company was doing really well and should continue doing.

  1) The first group compiled a list of three items. They spent 90% of their allotted time discussing, clarifying, summarizing, and prioritizing the items on their list. A leader was not selected as the group felt quite comfortable *sharing* the leadership role.

  2) The second group produced a list of ten items, but spent 90% of their time simply compiling the list. One member of the group took immediate control of the paper and markers and personally wrote the list, only asking for input from his teammates after he had created the list. During the debriefing, the self-appointed leader confessed that his need for structure and control always propelled him to "grab the markers."

3) While both groups took the same amount of time, one participant from the second group observed that the "leader" of group two could have compiled and distributed the list on his own and given his teammates some free time.

Not surprisingly, the first group indicated a greater sense of *ownership* of and willingness to implement those activities that worked really well. Interacting with others based on *our* needs rather than *theirs* can weaken commitment and reduce follow through.

What Others Have Observed

Employee engagement and its impact on employee productivity is a major topic of interest in many organizations. Employees who spend their time searching websites like Careerbuilder®, Monster.com®, and others for better employment opportunities may still be employees but are certainly not actively engaged in the organization's mission. The esteemed Gallup® organization claims that, "70% of American workers are 'not engaged' or 'actively disengaged.'" Gallup uses its Q12 Survey to measure employee engagement and its impact on the outcomes that matter most to a business. More than 25 million employees worldwide have participated in the Gallup surveys.

Gallup's *2013 State of the American Workplace, Employee Engagement Insights for U.S. Business Leaders* reports: "engaged employees are the lifeblood of their organizations. Work units in the top 25% of Gallup Q12 Client Database, their proprietary twelve question survey, have significantly higher productivity, profitability, and customer ratings, less turnover and absenteeism and fewer safety incidents than those in the bottom 25%. Organizations with an average of 9.3 engaged employees for every actively disengaged employee in 2010-2011 experienced 147% higher earnings per share (EPS) compared with their competition in 2011-2012. In contrast, those with an average of 2.6 engaged employees for every actively disengaged employee experienced 2% lower EPS compared with their competition during the same time period."

Gallup found that the manner in which managers and leaders interact with employees impacts the employees' level of engagement: "…managers who focus on their employees' strengths can practically eliminate active disengagement…." Managers must also actively find ways to connect with each employee: "…each person has different needs and expectations…every interaction has the potential to influence an employee's engagement…."

Needs + Expectations = Motivational Drivers

The recurring theme throughout this book is *in order to bring out the best in others; one must "treat them as they want to be treated."* Treating someone primarily as *we* want to be treated may be a recipe for disaster—just ask Mrs. Orr. It stands to reason that a "one size fits all" perspective has its shortcomings. Each person is unique. Each person has their own set of needs and expectations or motivational drivers. These motivational drivers are powerful determinants of an individual's behavior.

Whether we are discussing enhancing employee engagement, unleashing another's greatness, or providing an environment where one can become all they are capable of becoming, the bottom line is this: managers and leaders play a crucial role.

Consider this example. Until six months ago, Charles was an actively engaged employee. Under his previous supervisor he thrived. He was in his zone. He was flourishing. Now he wants to quit.

Charles' job duties had not changed but his immediate supervisor had. The new supervisor tended to tell and not ask. He wasn't a very effective listener, and he preferred to "help" employees by frequently instructing them on how to do their jobs. Charles felt constrained and disrespected. His performance slipped. He lost the excitement he'd once felt for his job and the organization. In short, he'd become disengaged.

When he started to complain about his supervisor to other employees, he found some support. His complaints soon began to stir up discontent among his peers. At that point Charles was "actively" disengaged.

Charles' supervisor was on the verge of firing him. The entire situation had spiraled out of hand. Charles contacted Carl for advice, and Carl suggested he take the **UMMD™** self-assessment.

Charles' **UMMD™** Report indicated that the following motivational drivers were significant to him:

Table 1.2
Charles' Significant Motivational Drivers

TOPICS	CHARLES
HOW TO WORK WITH ME	Impose a minimum of routine
HOW TO TALK TO ME	Be positive and reassuring
BIGGEST MISTAKES YOU CAN MAKE WITH ME	Not listening to my explanations
HOW TO INCENTIVIZE ME	Provide tangible incentives
MOTIVATING ME FOR BEST PERFORMANCE	Give plenty of opportunities for me to act on my own initiative

Unfortunately, his supervisor was not aware of Charles' motivational drivers. In almost every interaction the supervisor "crushed" one of them. The supervisor wasn't a bad person; he was probably managing based primarily on his own needs or using an approach that had been successful for him with others in the past. His awareness of Charles' specific needs was nonexistent. The organization hadn't yet instituted a protocol where employees were encouraged to share and discuss their **UMMD™** Reports with others. Charles concluded that he'd be better off in another environment and resigned.

About a year ago, Kim, a successful commissioned sales professional, accepted a position as a salaried sales manager. Almost immediately, Kim's performance leveled off. After a recent discussion with Carl, it became apparent to Kim that one of the main issues was the salary.

Kim had always been energized by having to start over each month to earn her worth. The fixed salary, although desired by some, was an impediment to Kim. Her **UMMD™** Report indicated that she preferred an at risk compensation program. The salaried compensation program was not a motivator for her. She decided to ask her CEO to change her compensation arrangement to be better aligned with her motivational drivers.

A recent television advertisement by the company that sponsors the Discover credit card proclaims, "We treat you like you treat you!" Surely, managers and leaders should consider doing the same.

As previously mentioned, Dr. Tony Alessandra's Platinum Rule of Leadership states: "Treat others as they want to be treated." Implicit in this definition is a requirement for both self-awareness and awareness of others. If one is aware of another's motivational drivers, they can be taken into consideration when deciding how best to interact with that person. Understanding the motivational drivers of another person allows you to consider a greater number of options for more effectively interacting with them.

How to Read This Book

While this book follows the typical format of sequential chapters, we recognize that not everyone learns in a linear, sequential fashion. Therefore, we encourage you to simply pick up the book, open to any page and read a paragraph or two. If what you read is interesting, then keep reading. If not, pick another part of the book and review a paragraph or two.

At some point, the concepts of the book will grab your interest, and that interest will guide you the rest of the way. Some of the points in this book may touch you in a way that enhances your self-awareness. Other points may help you to better understand someone else. This enhanced awareness, whether of self or of others, is life enriching. Life *changing*.

Reflection

1. To what extent are people treating you like you want to be treated?

2. Are others bringing out the best in you?

3. Are you bringing out the best in others?

CHAPTER 2:

WHY BE YOUR BEST?

Josh stepped back and gazed at what he'd done. Before him rested a finely crafted vase. On its base he'd proudly stamped *Crafted with care by Josh*. Three weeks ago, Josh had conceived the idea of the vase in his mind. He'd thought about it for days before he went to his home studio and began to work on it. Josh had labored hard for three hours to complete his project, and now it was done. He'd created this object with his hands. Its shape had flowed from his mind, but its essence was from his heart. This vase was part of Josh. It reflected his love for his work. It represented the combination of his God-given talent with clay and a simple potter's wheel. His finished product was indeed a work of art. A work of art because it was a work of love.

On the way to his office the next day, Josh thought about his feelings of accomplishment and pride from the previous night. Why, he wondered, did he get such a sense of fulfillment from working at his potter's wheel and so little satisfaction from his day job? What made the two activities so vastly different? He started compiling a list of differences: His job was rather structured. He was told what and how to do his daily tasks. There was no room for innovation and no recognition or reward for making suggestions on how to improve his work output. His hobby was nearly the opposite. He decided what he was going to do and how he'd do it. Thinking of better ways to do things and incorporating his own suggestions for improvements was rewarding to Josh. It energized him, made him feel worthwhile, and set him free. His day job was confining, restraining, and robbed him of his energy. Josh's day job limited his opportunities to be his best. The fit was just not right.

Alignment

What options are available if you find yourself in an unfulfilling situation similar to Josh's? Do you just grin and bear it? What could eventually happen to you as a person if the alignment between your authentic self and the situation you're in are in conflict? How long could you tolerate the stress caused by such a misalignment? How would such a misalignment impact those you care the about most? How would you cope with the hole created in your soul? Perhaps the best approach is not to answer these questions now but to reframe our thinking.

Lifestyle Goals

Let's start first with your Lifestyle Goals. What is important to you? Is it family, friends, health, spiritual matters, intellectual pursuits, community service, or wealth? Or it is some combination thereof? Whatever you decide, that's your starting point. Focus on how you want to spend your life. What do you love to do? What makes you feel like *you*? What puts you in your zone? Clayton M. Christensen, is his thought-provoking book *How Will You Measure Your Life?* challenges us to think about how we'd spend our life if we knew we were going to die in three years. What might we start doing? What might we stop doing? What might we do differently? How might we invest our time? Would it be more time with loved ones or more time for personal pursuits? Or both?

Each person must decide the proper course for them. Some of us made that decision years ago. Others are struggling with that decision today. And, unfortunately, some of us don't even realize that there's a choice.

William James, a giant of a thinker in the field of psychology, recognized that one's concepts, perceptions, ideas, and ways of thinking can help or hinder how we frame situations. His most powerful message was that a person can alter their way of living by altering their way of thinking.

Below are listed some typical examples of Martin's and Carl's life-style goals from recent years. Note, that each uses a format that fits their preferences.

Some of Martin's recent lifestyle goals follow:

Fitness Goals:
- Target weight: 175 lbs.
- Target body fat: 9%
- Do at least one yoga class per week

Thinking Goals:
- Annual one day strategic thinking retreat
- Quarterly half-day strategic thinking retreat
- Weekly activity plan for the coming week

Renewal Goals:
- Observe the Sabbath each week
- One week vacation to Alaska
- Four weekend getaway trips

Relational Goals:
- Weekly dates with wife
- Daddy-daughter dates at least twice a month
- Father-son adventures at least twice a month

Financial Goals:
- Establish and review family budget monthly
- Publish more articles nationally

Some of Carl's recent lifestyle goals follow:

Spiritual Grounding and Growth:
- Daily time in prayer and meditation
- Annual participation in a multi-day silent spiritual retreat

Family:
- Spend more quality time with wife

- Support wife's creative talent emotionally and financially
- Help daughter and son-in-law realize their dreams

Recharge Batteries:
- First class cruise to Greece with wife
- Attend three or four embassy dinners per year
- Increase activities with Washington Performing Arts Society, The National Gallery of Art, and The Kennedy Center

Health:
- Continue with weight control plan
- Exercise/walk three or four times a week
- Quarterly and annual check-ups with all doctors

Responsible Wealth:
- Maintain Whole Life Insurance coverage at maximum Human Life Value
- Save one-third of gross income
- Eliminate all short term debt

Intellectual Development:
- Read at least three books per month
- Participate in at least one monthly webinar

So, what do you want out of your life? Start with a clean slate. What makes you happy? What fulfills you? What are you best at doing or being? Do you have overarching life goals that would fit into one of the following categories? (Note: We define a goal as *a broad, general statement of a desired end result.* For instance: to maintain a healthy lifestyle, to achieve financial independence, or to spend more quality time with loved ones.) Describe two or three of your major life goals for each category.

Spiritual: Awareness, meaning of life, values, principles
Family/Relationships: Love, family, friendships, special groups
Health/Fitness: Weight, energy, exercise, stress management
Intellectual: Expansion of knowledge, increased understanding, wisdom
Community Service: Helping others, giving back, paying forward
Wealth: Accumulation, protection, enjoyment, sharing

Now think of your answers to the areas above as a centering compass. If your responses really reflect your lifestyle preferences and goals, then what type of activity, task, job, profession, career, or calling might you be attracted to? After all, each of us needs a way to finance our Lifestyle Goals. What do you daydream about? What kinds of activities do you enjoy? What ideas, people, challenges, etc. absorb your attention and energize you? What questions do you find stimulating? What are you passionate about? What are you proficient in? The intersection of your passion and talent is where you'll find your uniqueness.

Appreciating Your Uniqueness

Each person has value. Each person has been given talents, skills, and abilities that make them unique. People tend to be uniquely great at a few things, good at many other things, average at still more things, and poor at a few things. If your job requires you to sit behind a desk all day working with numbers and not interacting with people and your uniqueness is to be out interacting with people then you have a problem. Your uniqueness is not being utilized. If your job requires you to be creative and you prefer to be involved in solving specific, concrete issues then your uniqueness is not being utilized. If you prefer to use your initiative in performing your job and your supervisor is a micro-manager, then your uniqueness is not being utilized. If your coworker is not cooperative and you're a very collaborative individual, then your uniqueness is not being utilized. If your....*You can fill in the blank with your own example.*

Consistently operating out of alignment with your uniqueness deprives you of the opportunity to be your best. You're like a fish out of water. A fish that someone has decided should do something other than swim. Perhaps they want the fish to learn how to climb trees. It's not going to happen! People, like fish, can't thrive in situations that don't honor their uniqueness. Ignore a person's uniqueness, and you rob them of their greatness.

What is your uniqueness? Do you like working alone or with others? Or both? Do you enjoy work that requires long hours of concentration or work that offers variety? Or both? Do you prefer to plan out your work and then work your plan, or do you prefer to get started and then shape your plan as you go along? Or sometimes do you prefer a little of both? There are questions that we each need to ask ourselves to discover our true self.

Try this exercise: Create two columns. Label one column *Things I do extremely well* and the other column *Why I am passionate about this*. Spend quality time thinking about your responses. Consider both personal and professional activities that you do extremely well. Brainstorm with yourself. Think about what you loved doing as a child. Are you still involved in some of these activities? When you are most happy, what are you doing? Jot down some of your more important ideas under the *Things I do extremely well* column.

Think carefully about *why* you enjoy doing these activities and list these thoughts under the *Why I am passionate about this* column. Your passion statements are crucial. Your passion is the fuel that propels your activities. Your passion energizes you. Your passion sustains you. Your passion gives meaning to your efforts. Your passion is your *why*, and it determines how you are who you are. Try to list four to six items under each heading. Share your list with someone who can help you check for blind spots. Then take those items and try writing a "Unique Me" statement. An example follows:

THINGS I DO EXTREMELY WELL	WHY I AM PASSIONATE ABOUT THIS
Listen well for the real meaning behind a person's words	Want to truly understand the person
Organizing and following a work plan	Enjoy the sense of accomplishment
Adaptable to changing priorities	Challenges me to grow
Collaborating with others	Like being part of a team

Here is a sample "Unique Me" statement based on the above. *I am passionate about working with others to plan and complete a task or project that involves understanding and adapting to changing situations.* Your statement should reflect a combination of your passions and your talents. This combination of passions and talents is your sweet spot. That's where you want to be if you're to be your best, unleash your greatness, and become all that you're capable of becoming.

Be Yourself

Oscar Wilde noted, *Be Yourself: everybody else is already taken.* Once you have clarified your Lifestyle Goals and created your "Unique Me" statement of passions and abilities, you can relax and just be yourself. Being your best self is the easiest way to be authentic. You're unique and therefore special. Focus on what makes *you* special. You may be great at planning parties, but not so great at tennis. You may be great at streamlining work processes, but not so great at repairing things. You may have a quick wit and a sense of humor but not do well at adding up a column of numbers in your head. Accept yourself for who you are, a person with unique talents and abilities. Appreciate your specialness. George Eliot said it well *It's never too late to be what you might have been.*

It's important that others recognize, understand, and embrace our specialness. There's a powerful fable entitled "The Animal School" by George Reavis that might help illustrate this point.

> Once upon a time, the animal kingdom decided to do something meaningful to help solve the world's problems and to cross-train its members. It organized a school and adopted an activity curriculum of running, climbing, swimming and flying. To make it easier to administer the curriculum, each animal was required to take all the subjects.

The duck was an excellent swimmer but nearly failed at running. Since he was a slow runner, he had to stay after school to practice. His webbed feet became so badly worn that he dropped to an average in his swimming class. But average was quite acceptable, so nobody worried about his performance—except the duck.

The rabbit quickly jumped to the top of the class in running but had a nervous breakdown because of so much make up work in swimming. The rabbit never quite got the hang of swimming under water despite extra attention from his instructors.

The squirrel excelled in climbing but encountered constant frustration studying flying because the teacher made him work from the ground up instead of from the top down. He developed charley horses from overexertion and received a "C" in climbing and a "D" in running, two activities he had previously excelled in.

The eagle was a problem student in all his classes and was severely disciplined for being a nonconformist. In tree climbing competition, he was the first to the top of the tree but insisted on using his own means of getting there instead of following the instructions outlined in the textbook.

The prairie dog stayed out of school and just sat at home and complained because digging and burrowing classes weren't offered.

Moral: Each creature in the animal kingdom has its own "uniqueness," its own set of capabilities at which it excels naturally and effortlessly. A duck is a duck. It is built to swim not to run. If it is forced into a mold that does not fit, frustration and disappointment ensue, and mediocrity and defeat often result.

This story was written when George Reavis was the Assistant Superintendent of the Cincinnati Public Schools in the 1940's.

In closing, perhaps the words of Jessie Belle Rittenhouse (1869–1948) will inspire you:

I bargained with Life for a penny,
And Life would pay no more,
However I begged at evening
When I counted my scanty store;
For Life is a just employer,
He gives you what you ask,
But once you have set the wages,
Why, you must bear the task.
I worked for a menial's hire,
Only to learn, dismayed,
That any wage I had asked of Life,
Life would have paid.

Do you really think this poem is about wages? Try substituting other words such as happiness, fulfillment, or self-actualization.

Reflection

1. What lifestyle goals are important to you?

2. What do you do extremely well?

3. Why are you passionate about what you do extremely well?

4. What is your "Unique Me" statement?

"Coming together is a beginning; keeping together is progress; working together is success"

— HENRY FORD

CHAPTER 3:

HOW TO WORK WITH ME

Let's take a little journey together. To begin, think back to the last time you interviewed for a job with a new employer. Okay, we know, for some of you that may seem like forever ago. For others, it may seem like yesterday. Dust off those cobwebs if you need to and take some time to consider the process and the purpose. The company was trying to size you up and see if you were a fit for the position, while you were seeking to present your best self and sell them on the idea of choosing you for the job. If you've ever participated in either side of the interview process, you know that it's a very inexact science.

The process typically starts with submitting a resume. There it is— your life story on one or two pages, including your education, experiences, and accomplishments. Maybe you had your hobbies listed for a personal touch as well. With these quick facts, the interviewer will size you up and see if you pass the first hurdle in the process. From the resume, the interviewer can only really see if you have the right education and work experience for the job. A resume with typos or other errors will usually end up in the NO pile. To learn more about the candidate, a business will typically do a phone interview or maybe move right on to a face to face interview.

While some companies have elaborate hiring processes with multiple interviews, personality tests, or other detailed evaluations, most employers still make a lot of gut decisions after one or two interviews. Unfortunately, our gut isn't always the best filter, and the result is a bad fit between employer and employee. As an interviewee, you probably answered a number of questions about yourself and your career. Think about what the interviewer really learned about you. For example, did they learn about your preferred work environment? Did they figure out what really motivates you? Were they able to learn about the best ways to communicate with you? For most people, the answer is no.

Too often, we don't really understand these things about ourselves. We lack that level of self-awareness. We may not understand if we prefer structured versus unstructured work environments. We may not know that we prefer detailed instructions versus general direction. The list could continue. If we are not self-aware, then we'll likely find ourselves either frustrated or enjoying our work without understanding why. If we don't understand these things about ourselves, then we'll have a very hard time guiding others in how to treat us the way we need to be treated.

If our needs as a human being aren't being met then the result will be what we refer to as "negative stress behavior." For example, I (Martin) prefer not to be overscheduled. I like to have time to process complex issues and come up with thoughtful conclusions. When I have too many deadlines at one time, I become very quiet, focused, and reserved. That is not my normal personality. For years, I fell into this pattern and my colleagues wondered what was wrong with me. Finally, I became aware of this negative stress behavior, and so I began to forewarn my colleagues and let them know in advance that everything was fine.

Let's continue our journey together. So you've made it through the gauntlet and got the job. Congratulations! Now, think back to your very first day of work. It probably started with some type of orientation. For some companies, this can be a multiday or even week process. For others, it may be all of about an hour. However long or short, you probably spent some time filling out some paperwork—stacks of official looking papers. Maybe company policies and procedures were provided for your review. Perhaps you learned about the benefits the company offered.

Maybe in today's high tech world you watched some videos about things your employer wanted you to know.

Some organizations use the orientation process to share about their "DNA"—their core values. They want their employees to understand the "why" of the organization and the vision for the company's future. For the new hire, the orientation process can be like drinking from a fire hose. It becomes a blur of information, facts, and forms.

As you began the new job, you likely had new teammates, a new boss, and maybe new people to manage. Success is never a solo event. Our success is tied to how we interact with others and function as a team. Being a new employee on a team can be like a flashback to school days and being the new kid. We have to navigate these new relationships and start to learn people's skills, abilities, personalities, and styles.

What is interesting about the orientation process at most companies is that the information flow is usually a one-way street. In other words, the business is flooding the new hire with information, but the organization is not taking time to learn more about the individual. In the interview process, we share a lot of information about ourselves. However, the questions usually stop there. Perhaps we should rethink that. Maybe orientation should be a balanced process of orienting the individual to the company and the company orienting to the individual.

Problems Caused By Failing To Work Together

What happens when we fail to learn how to work with each other in the workplace? BIG PROBLEMS! Sometimes they take a while to surface, other times the impact is immediate. Let us tell you about James. James is a friend of mine (Martin) whom I've known for a long time. He's a very smart and diligent worker. When you give him a difficult project, he'll think through all of the issues thoroughly and deliver great results. However, for James to perform at his best, he needs context for the project and a reasonable timeline. Several years ago, he took a job with a large organization after an extensive interview process. He beat out many qualified candidates to land the job.

After a surprisingly brief orientation, he was assigned to a department and team. His team leader was a seasoned veteran who had a "sink or swim" philosophy. James was shown his new office and found several files on his desk. His boss wasn't around, so James began to review the files. He sat for hours trying to figure out what he was supposed to do. Later in the day, his new boss briefly stopped by and told him to review the files and take care of the projects outlined in the files—no context, no explanation. His boss said, "By the way, I need these projects completed by the end of the week."

James took the files home and worked late into the night trying to figure out what needed to be done. Unfortunately, the data was incomplete, and James had more questions than answers. The next day, he went in to see his boss, seeking a better understanding of what needed to be done. His boss was on the phone and waved him off to come back later. James was persistent and eventually was able to speak with his boss. His boss was agitated because James wanted to have a detailed understanding of the projects and basically told him to "figure it out!" There he was—two days on the job with several large projects, a tight deadline, and very little information. His boss went out of town the next day, and James was able to speak with some colleagues about his problem.

James soon learned that this was the boss' typical style and that James shouldn't expect much help or explanation of his assignments. The culture of the boss' department reflected his "sink or swim" attitude. The reality began to set in for James that he'd made a big mistake. After another day or two of thinking through his dilemma, James decided to quit his job. He was wise enough to know that he wouldn't thrive in that work environment. When James told his boss that he was quitting, his boss was shocked. He boss thrived on deadlines and was a very unorganized person. He couldn't relate to James' need for context, structure, and reasonable deadlines. That company lost a great employee as James went on to a very successful career with a competitor.

While James' story is an extreme example, the lack of understanding about how to work together is a silent killer in most organizations. When people's needs are not being met in the organization, we see dysfunctional teams, poor performance, and CYA (Cover Your Assets) type behavior. While some people have a natural ability to know how to work with others, that's the exception rather than the norm. For most, it takes time, effort, and experience to learn how to work best with others.

Once we become aware of our needs and those of others, we can accelerate through this process to create high performance teams and organizations. However, it takes a high degree of intentionality and willingness to look at ourselves honestly to accomplish this. I (Martin) was reminded of the importance of being self-aware when I recently joined a new company. For years, I'd been my own boss and led my own company. However, I decided to merge my consulting practice into a larger organization.

When I started, I was assigned an executive assistant to assist me. I came in one day and found a copy of Dr. Gary Chapman's and Dr. Paul White's book *The Five Languages of Appreciation in the Workplace* in my chair. Whoa! I wondered whether I'd missed something. Was she trying to give me a message? Was I off to a bad start as a boss? I've managed many people during my career, but I began to question myself. Once we talked, my fears were allayed as my assistant had read the book and knew I'd enjoy it. This led to a detailed discussion between us about the importance of showing appreciation and what her "language" was for best receiving appreciation. We both learned a lot about how to work with each other that day and have been committed to making sure we're optimizing our ability to work together.

Not long after my learning experience with my new assistant, I had a similar experience with one of my new partners. I'd known my new business partner for a number of years, but we'd never formally worked together. We began to have some communication problems and our friendship became strained. What I realized was that even though we thought we knew each other, we'd taken for granted some things about each other and didn't realize there were some deep needs that weren't being met. I realized that I was being a poor communicator, and my partner valued good communication. Similarly, my colleague was a quick thinker, and I needed time to process complex decisions. Through our discussion, we were able to diffuse a negative situation and find a much better way to work successfully together.

A Solution

In the workplace, there is an obvious knowledge gap that occurs between individuals involving knowing the best way to work together. While people usually stumble their way to figuring out a lot of these nuances over time, countless hours of frustration and lost productivity occur as this process unfolds. We believe there's a better way. The *UMMD*™ self-assessment was created to address these types of problems. It allows colleagues to close this knowledge gap and break through the mystery of determining how to best work together. The report raises your own self-awareness, which is a critical first step in the process. It can also be shared with your teammates, your boss, and even people you manage. By sharing this information you inspire communication. You are able to have a direct and honest conversation with your colleagues about how you can work together in a way that meets your deepest needs and benefits the organization. The report can even be used in the interview process to determine if prospective employees and organizations are matched up for success.

Below is a sample of the feedback from one individual's report. Do any of the items resonate with you?

- Be direct and straightforward with me
- Don't constantly force group interaction on me
- Incentivize me using generalized and more abstract rewards
- Offer me challenging assignments.
- Give me plenty of time for complex or difficult decisions
- Be sure to offer me concrete, material rewards
- Don't overschedule me
- Encourage my natural self-confidence; where possible, offer discreet support if I encounter failure
- Offer me opportunities to express my individuality

Conclusion

The ability to work effectively together is critical to our success as individuals and as organizations. We know that through the process of increased self-awareness and intentional communication with colleagues that performance can be improved and that people can enjoy a more productive work environment. We encourage you to take the first step and consider your own needs as an individual. Reflect on the sample statements above. Ask your friends and colleagues when you seem to perform your best. As you gain these insights, share them with your colleagues and seek to understand how to work with them. Ask and listen carefully as they describe their needs and preferred work environments. The time invested in learning how to work together has a significant long term payoff. Start the habit today of being much more attuned to your own work styles and those of people around you. You won't regret it!

"People who work together will win, whether it is against complex football defenses, or the problems of modern society."

—VINCE LOMBARDI

Reflection

1. How would you describe a great day at work?

2. How would you describe a not so great day at work?

3. What are some of the major factors that determine whether or not you have a great day at work?

"I know you believe you understand what you think I said, but what you heard is not what I meant."

—ATTRIBUTED TO VARIOUS INDIVIDUALS

CHAPTER 4:

HOW TO TALK TO ME

Eric was perplexed. He thought he'd considered every suggestion Janet had made with regard to the Arnold project. Yet, in the project review meeting with Janet that morning, she seemed irritated. She kept insisting that he wasn't being cooperative, wasn't paying attention to her recommendations, and was causing the project to fall behind schedule. When Eric tried to explain the decisions he'd made and the actions he'd taken, Janet folded her arms and stared at him. Then she informed Eric that she'd already told him exactly what to do for the Arnold project and as far as she was concerned, Eric had ignored all of her instructions.

Sandra and Debra had always considered themselves an excellent event planning team. They had collaborated on so many assignments that they felt they each always knew what the other was thinking or about to say, so they never felt compelled to spend much time reviewing the plans or discussing the details. Sandra, however, was scheduled for surgery in two weeks, and Peter was stepping in to take her place. Almost from the start Peter felt he was being kept in the dark. Neither Sandra nor Debra would tell him very much about the next assignment—the annual awards banquet for one of their major corporate clients. He felt like they were communicating in some secret language.

Bill was being considered for a team leader position that had recently opened up. Management thought Bill did an excellent job of keeping them informed and considered him to be a good problem solver. Management thought that he might develop into a good team leader and gave him an opportunity to test-drive the position for six weeks. After just three weeks, management informed Bill that while his upward communication skills were great, his failure to engage his team members in everyday work situations was causing the department to fall behind.

As the examples above demonstrate, effective communication is not easy. Sometimes we incorrectly think we know what the other person is trying to communicate and don't ask clarifying questions. Including a newcomer in our inner circle of communications breaks up comfortable, and often effective, habits of behavior. Too often, we expect others to change instead of being willing to change ourselves. Sometimes, communication problems occur when someone assumes a new role in the organization. Every role change involves changes in attitude, perspective, behavior, and communication. Not recognizing this can lead to unpleasant results.

In contrast, consider the following example:

Tom was ecstatic. Two weeks ago he'd instructed Lisa, the graphic designer, to create a logo for one of their new offerings. He recalled that Lisa had spent considerable time asking him about his color preferences, logo usage, impact, and how much of a "wow" factor he wanted the image to have. Lisa's inquisitive approach helped Tom clarify some of his thoughts and encouraged him to be more specific in communicating his vision for the proposed logos. As he looked at the proposed logos, Tom realized that he liked all three examples. Each logo, he thought, reflected exactly what he and Lisa had discussed. Tom realized that he was going to have a difficult time selecting just one.

What Happened?

Sometimes, such as in the case of Eric and Janet, one might perceive instructions as suggestions. Obviously that was Eric's perception. Janet, on the other hand, considered her instructions as non-negotiable directives.

This initial difference in perceptions was never rectified. The gap in understanding led to a gap in expected results and probably a further breakdown in their relationship. Neither Eric nor Janet was happy.

The case of Tom and Lisa ended on a more positive note probably because of the clarification discussion on the front end of the logo project. Lisa and Tom got involved in an interactive process that strengthened their level of understanding of what was expected and what was to be delivered. This led to Lisa being more engaged in her tasks and more productive. Lisa was happy. Tom was happy.

The example involving Sandra, Debra, and Peter provides insight into the impact of not adjusting one's communication style to include others. Sandra and Debra seemed to click on what they thought, said, and meant. Peter, on the other hand, didn't have that connection and apparently Sandra and Debra didn't feel compelled to alter what worked for them to a style that would work for them *and* Peter. Peter was unhappy.

In the last example above, Bill's upward communication effectiveness worked well for him in his role as an individual contributor. In his role as a team leader he struggled with adapting his one-on-one style to effectively communicating to a one-on-group style with his team members. This negatively impacted his team members' level of engagement and productivity. Bill wasn't happy, his team members weren't happy, and his manager wasn't happy.

Face-to-Face Communication Effectiveness Formula

Dr. Albert Mehrabian is credited with developing the frequently labeled 7%-38%-55% formula for determining the effectiveness of a face-to-face spoken communication exchange involving feelings and attitude. Most sources shorten the formula to the following— The total impact of a face-to-face communication exchange is composed of:

7% Words spoken
38% Tone of voice, pitch, inflection
55% Nonverbal facial expression and body language

One must be careful in interpreting this formula. The 7% weight of the words spoken doesn't mean that words aren't important. They are. The words spoken may carry less weight in the total impact of the message when there's inconsistency or ambiguity between the spoken word, tone of voice, and/or the nonverbal component. In these situations, especially when the spoken message pertains to feelings and attitudes, the tone of voice and nonverbal components often convey the stronger message and, in effect, diminish that of the words said.

For example, once, I (Carl) arrived home nearly two hours later than I'd promised. My wife was rather distant when I greeted her. I then asked her if she was upset with me. Her reply, through clenched teeth, with a high-pitched voice and dagger-throwing eyes was: "No, I am not upset!" There was no doubt that she was quite upset. Her words lost all meaning when coupled with her tone of voice and the anger in her eyes.

Mehrabian's formula is quite useful if one remembers it applies primarily to face-to-face verbal communication exchanges involving feelings and attitudes. The formula wasn't intended to measure the total impact of face-to-face exchanges not involving feelings and attitudes. If I ask a salesperson the price of a shirt, his/her reply of $75.00 has all the meaning needed for a successful face-to-face communication exchange.

So much of one-on-one communication exchanges today are via email or text messaging. In these media, the words used are the primary component of the message. Aside from the use of smiley faces or all caps, there's no opportunity to convey tone of voice or nonverbal behaviors. Some written emails and text messages leave no doubt as to the writer's attitude or feelings.

For our purposes, the essential point is to be aware of the three components to a face-to-face exchange when it occurs. If there's an inconsistency between the words spoken and either the tone of voice or nonverbal behavior, the words will carry very little weight.

Try this with a friend. Tell your friend that you're exploring how well people listen to instructions and ask him/her if they would be willing to help you with an experiment. Looking straight into their eyes, ask your friend to touch his/her chin with his/her pointer finger. However, as you say this, touch your cheek with your pointer finger. If your friend follows your nonverbal message, he or she will likely point his/her finger to his/her cheek instead of chin.

The point of this simple experiment isn't to fool or embarrass anyone. The point is to demonstrate that our actions speak louder than our words—just what Mehrabian's formula suggests when there are inconsistencies between the spoken word and the nonverbal behavior.

Communication Styles

Most of us interact with a number of different people on a daily basis. Some in our work, others as we go about our daily living. Each person we interact with has different perceptions and perspectives, different opinions, different values and beliefs, and different communication styles and communication needs. Once we have a face-to-face exchange with another person, we can usually gain some understanding about how they prefer to communicate with others. The challenge is in determining how another person prefers communication. One's outward behavior is not always in alignment with one's inner needs—that is, how someone prefers others to talk to them.

Direct vs. Indirect

Some people are very direct communicators. They tend to be straightforward and to the point. Usually there's no doubt about the message sent. Others are more indirect. They aren't as clear or concise. They may even be a little evasive or ambiguous in their responses. People with direct styles might prefer others to be direct with them or not. And the same goes for people with indirect styles. It's helpful to think of the direct-indirect style as continuum. One style isn't considered right or wrong, better or worse. They're simply different. A communication style breakdown can occur when one's preference for how they would prefer others to communicate with them goes consistently unmet.

For example, Jenny is a direct communicator. Her communication exchanges are frank, concise and to the point. She typically uses a "telling" style, and her need is for others to do the same. Jenny's focus is more about the message. Wilbur is an indirect communicator. He tends to communicate in an "asking" style. His communication exchanges are less specific and more general. Wilbur's focus is more about the person and how they might react to what he says. He often is seen as being somewhat evasive. He has a need for others to communicate with him in the same indirect "asking" or less direct style. When Jenny uses her direct style with Wilbur, his needs aren't met. He may feel disrespected or threatened. However, when Wilbur uses his indirect style of communication with Jenny, she may find herself frustrated that he won't get to the point.

Private vs. Group

Some people best receive information one-on-one. In contrast, others prefer to discuss matters in a group setting. For people who prefer private conversations, they may be reluctant to speak up in a group context or share their true opinions or thoughts.

For example, Douglas prefers one-on-one communication settings because he feels most comfortable giving or receiving information in this way. If Diane, his boss, simply asks for feedback in a group setting, then she won't have the benefit of Douglas' true thoughts on the issue at hand. For people who value private conversations, it's a way to show them you understand and appreciate them.

One can quickly conclude from the brief examples presented above that communicating isn't an easy thing to do. How people talk to us is important to us. Yet, some people will never learn our preferences by trial and error or by guessing our needs. Worse, they may assume that our communication needs are just like theirs and treat us accordingly.

Share and Discuss

A key feature of the **UMMD™** Report is that it provides the individual a personalized summary of how they prefer people to talk to them. We'll conclude this chapter with some real life examples. The statements below are personalized descriptions of individuals' communication preferences. Study them carefully. Consider whether there are any communication needs that you share with people in the examples. Do you see some that you've never thought about? Are you perplexed by any of them? Can you appreciate how unique some communication needs are?

Communication Preferences

- Be careful to show me a degree of respect. Don't be too abrupt.

- If the subject is important, talk to me alone.

- Get to the point. Don't worry too much about hurting my feelings.

- Be agreeable. Avoid confrontation with me.

- Keep irrelevant matters to an absolute minimum.

- Where possible, present the big idea to me first and then wait for a response before going into more detail. If there is a financial component to our discussions, emphasizes it freely, particularly where I will benefit personally.

- Try and frame the matter under discussion as something that I can achieve. Show me that you believe I can succeed.

- Asking me how I feel about the matter under discussion can generate more cooperation and yield significant insights for us both.

- Encourage me to think "outside the box" if you really want to engage my attention.

- Don't press me to come to any conclusion in our first conversation. Give me time to think it over.

- Emphasize those results which will offer benefits to others as well as me, or which will support my system of personal values.

Conclusion

Effective face-to-face communication is a constant challenge. Even if we select the correct words, use a consistent tone of voice, and align our nonverbal facial and gestural behavior our communication efforts may still falter. This is especially true if our communication style is inconsistent with the communication needs of the person we're interacting.

Discovering and understanding the best way to meet the communication needs of others is critical for effective interactions. Topic # 2 of the *UMMD™* Report provides an individual with the opportunity to review and confirm how they want others to talk to them. And, in addition, the report provides a framework where one's communication needs can be shared and discussed with others thus taking the guesswork out of how best to talk to them.

Reflection

1. How do you prefer to be talked to?

2. What style of communication from others makes you uncomfortable?

3. What style of communication from others brings out the best in you?

"Mistakes are the growing pains of wisdom."

— WILLIAM JORDAN

CHAPTER 5:
BIGGEST MISTAKES YOU CAN MAKE WITH ME

Our perspective of a situation, a person, and our needs and expectations influence every interaction we have with others. Our perception defines our reality. For example, two children were shown pictures of a man reading a book and of a man working on his automobile. When asked to describe the two pictures one child said, "The man working on the automobile is doing what my Dad does at work. He's a mechanic." The child then described the picture of the man reading the book as her Dad relaxing after a hard day at work. The second child, son of a professor, described the picture of the reader as his Dad at work as a professor and the other picture as his Dad relaxing on the weekend.

Each child's frame of reference was shaped by her/his environment and experience. Each chose to see the pictures in his/her own way. It was a way that made sense. A way that was comfortable and congruent. As human beings, we all tend to process information in a way that makes sense to us based on our own context. However, sometimes we can be inaccurate in our perceptions. Have you ever found yourself responding to a situation, a person, or an event with thoughts or words that made sense to you, only to later find out you were wrong?

What's Your Perspective?

Alice was angry. She was trying to explain to her brother Larry how upset she was about a situation at work that wasn't going well for her. Larry, who loathed conflict, listened to Alice's rants and then suggested that she "calm down" and not make any rash decisions about how she might handle her situation. Alice then proceeded to express her anger even louder as, clearly, in her view, Larry wasn't listening to her. He wasn't expressing support for her concerns and was, from her point of view, being patronizing. Alice concluded that it had been a mistake to confide in her brother. But the mistake wasn't hers it was Larry's. His approach to her situation was based more on his needs than on hers. In the future she wouldn't seek his advice on any matter, she decided.

Let's take a look at the Alice and Larry's exchange. How would it have been different if Larry had managed his own need for conflict avoidance and said something like: "I can see this situation is really upsetting to you. Please continue." Had Larry let Alice finish expressing her concerns she might have calmed down somewhat on her own. If so, then Larry could have helped Alice think through the various options open to her and the potential consequences of each. But Larry didn't do this.

Alice then decided to seek out Charles because he seemed to be nonjudgmental in his approach. Charles listened carefully without commenting. He allowed Alice to fully vent and didn't seem to mind all of the dramatic and emotional statements she made. When she was through, she thanked Charles. She told him that he'd been most helpful in assisting her in figuring out how to handle her situation. Charles smiled. He hadn't actually given her any advice. He'd just listened with understanding.

Many of us say and do well-meaning things only to discover later that our words or actions weren't received in the manner we intended. Each of us has our own set of needs and expectations surrounding how we want to be treated by others. When others don't know our needs and expectations we may feel mistreated and offended by their words or actions.

Paul was a sales manager in a financial services organization and keen on the concept of individual accountability. His unit was composed of six salespeople, each of whom looked to Paul for training and guidance as they grew in their careers. Paul liked to hold accountability meetings weekly with each person to help them stay focused on those activities that led to appointments with potential prospects. Five of the six salespeople seemed to thrive under this accountability concept. They scheduled and held appointments with prospective clients on a regular basis.

One salesperson, Earl, seemed resentful and tried to avoid the weekly accountability meetings. Paul asked one of his senior salespeople to speak with Earl. Earl seemed grateful for the opportunity to discuss his concerns with the senior salesperson. From Earl's perspective, he resented being questioned about his activities by Paul because they hardly knew each other. Earl didn't feel that Paul had made the effort to establish any rapport or relationship with him. Earl said he'd prefer to have had some quality time where he and Paul could just sit, talk, and get to know each other on a personal level first. He felt that developing a solid personal relationship was essential to establishing a solid business relationship.

When Paul was given this feedback from his senior salesperson, he became defensive. He rationalized that five of the six sales people he worked with were doing just fine with his accountability approach. He decided that his approach to sales management was appropriate and never entertained the thought that he might need to do something different to manage Earl effectively. Paul began to think that Earl wasn't a good fit for the organization. From then on, Paul avoided Earl. Six weeks later Earl left the company. In his exit interview with Human Resources, Earl said that he considered accountability without a relationship as harassment.

Jack and David had cubicles near each other and were both graphic designers. Both were creative, experienced professionals. Jack's worldview drove him to put in many hours of effort each day. He arrived early each morning, worked diligently throughout the day, and was often one of the last people to leave the office. Jack often made comments about other employees who didn't share the same work ethic he did. In fact, Jack felt he worked harder than anyone in the department.

David, on the other hand, had a different worldview when it came to work. He didn't agree with Jack's concept of "it's the amount of hours you put into the work." David's viewpoint was just the opposite. He believed it was "the amount of work you put into the hours" that was important. If he could create effective designs in a more efficient manner, he did so. He saw no logic in working long hours if he could get the job done in less time.

As long as they were peers in the organization, Jack and David tolerated each other. Their relationship wasn't necessarily a friendly one but they could work together when the project called for it. When Jack was promoted to supervisor of the graphic design group, the relationship changed drastically. Jack felt David was lazy and not engaged in his work. David felt Jack was a micro manager and spent most of his time being critical of David and of some of the other graphic designers.

David's response was to withdraw and not engage in any verbal discussions with Jack. This usually set Jack off, and he tended to rant and rave to other employees about how David wasn't contributing to the work of the department. In reality, David was contributing but not in the way that Jack thought he should. Jack was still hung up on the number of hours worked idea, and David was still focused on the amount of work he completed—regardless of the number of hours worked.

Jack tried to impose his worldview on David to no avail. Jack's attempt to measure David's performance by how "busy" he was during the day was a huge mistake. David was just not buying into it. Jack stayed frustrated most of the time. David retained his laid back posture. Jack's insistence on keeping timesheets was an insult to David. David's response was to ignore the weekly deadlines for submitting the timesheets. Both Jack and David displayed their least effective interpersonal behaviors when interacting with each other. They never did learn to work effectively together. Neither of them had much respect for the other.

Rather than forcing his work style and views on David, Jack could have taken a much more productive path. Great managers are great coaches. They know and understand the people on their team and help them be their very best. David had much to offer the team, but Jack missed the opportunity by being a micro-manager. Jack was never going to get greatness from David by forcing his will on him. Instead, he could have facilitated a conversation with David. He could have explained his viewpoint and tried to listen and understand David's point of view. This would have prevented the loss of a valued team member.

What Would You Do?

Helen held an important administrative position in the underwriting area of a large insurance company. Her job required careful attention to detail. She was expected to concentrate on one matter at a time for prolonged periods. She needed a work environment free from distractions and interruptions. Helen's work required the compiling of a great deal of information, followed by careful analysis. Then, and only then, was she expected to make a decision. When she was in her zone she performed at a very high level of output. Her work was accurate and complete. Utilizing only the information above about Helen, what would you do to help her be her best? Check off all of the actions you would take.

☐ Stop by Helen's desk daily to see how she was coming along with her projects.

☐ Minimize Helen's obligations to participate in staff meetings.

☐ Have Helen frequently train others to be focused and productive.

☐ Provide Helen a private office or quiet workspace.

Sally also held an important administrative position in the underwriting area of the same large insurance company. Her job, however, required her to be flexible and willing to address urgent matters as they occurred. She was known as the "fire fighter." Most critical issues were sent to her for resolution. She was expected to make quick but sound decisions with limited information. Utilizing only the information above about Sally, what would you do to help her be her best? Check off all of the actions you would take.

☐ Provide Sally quality data for her decisions.

☐ Provide Sally a lengthy policy manual to guide her decisions.

☐ Review each of Sally's decisions with her.

☐ Promote Sally to manage other people making similar decisions.

Reflection

1. In your life today is there someone who doesn't understand your unique motivational drivers?

2. Do you have a worldview that is significantly different from that of your boss? Best friend? Trusted coworker?

3. How are you dealing with this difference? Have you tried discussing your different perspectives with each other?

The **UMMD™** Report has a section on "The Biggest Mistakes You Can Make With Me." When we were preparing to write this book, we devoted some quality time to sharing and discussing each other's reports. The "biggest mistakes you can make with me" topic was particularly revealing. It became obvious very quickly that both of us, Carl and Martin, have strengths that, if imposed on the other, could create tension. Thankfully, the sharing and discussion of the various items in our respective reports highlighted these potential stressors and helped us to avoid making big mistakes with each other.

Interpreting the Needs of Others

We will have many important interactions with others where we won't have the benefit of the **UMMD™** Report with which to frame a discussion. How can we use our life experiences to help us avoid making big mistakes with others? While not as complete or as accurate as the report, here are a few suggestions from our life experiences that might help you think through your interactions.

You've developed an idea for a product that will eliminate roaming charges for data usage while traveling. You've tested the concept with several respected technology companies and now you're scheduled to meet individually with some key decision makers.

Situation 1: You're scheduled to meet with an individual who you know to be a perfectionist. He's careful and precise in his speech.

The biggest mistakes you should avoid are being disorganized, not being prepared, and not having the facts. What other mistakes would you want to avoid? Use the space below to record your comments.

Situation 2: Your next meeting is with an individual known to be enthusiastic, friendly, and political.

The biggest mistakes you should avoid are, trying to control the conversation, being cold and distant, and going into a lot of detail. What other mistakes would you want to avoid? Use the space below to record your comments.

Situation 3: Your third meeting is with an individual who is strong-willed, decisive, and strictly business.

The biggest mistakes you should avoid are not being clear about your purpose, talking too much, and appearing disorganized. What other mistakes would you want to avoid? Use the space below to record your comments.

Was it helpful to think about each of the three situations and to try adding your own mistakes to avoid? We hope so. As you can see it takes practice to get it right. First, one has to make an effort to learn, understand, and appreciate the needs and expectations of others. Second, one has to have sufficient self-awareness to recognize how one's usual behavior may create stress for others. Third, one has to be flexible enough to adjust one's usual behavior to fit the situation. Some of us can adjust our behavior for short periods of time and not feel too uncomfortable. Others may be able to adjust for longer periods. In either case, we certainly cannot expect the other person to change their needs just to satisfy our preferences for how we want to interact.

Reflection

Not all of our interactions are one-on-one.

1. What would you do if you were making a presentation to the three individuals referenced in the situations above? Visualize the meeting. You're presenting to them as a group. You know what your strengths are. You believe in your product idea. You have confidence in your communication skills. You realize that it's not about you. It's about them. And each of them is uniquely different.

2. How would you shape your presentation to address the various and possibly conflicting needs?

3. How could you be sure that in satisfying one person's needs you didn't create stress or tension for another person?

"It never made much sense to me to reward an employee for perfect attendance by giving them a day off from work."

— CARL HICKS

CHAPTER 6:

HOW TO INCENTIVIZE ME?

I (Martin) grew up in an entrepreneurial family. My father owned a furniture store so I grew up working in the family business. Fresh out of college, I cofounded a small business which operated private and public tennis facilities. Our paycheck was whatever was left in the bank account at the end of the month after paying our employees and our bills. While there was not much security in this arrangement, I thrived on the challenge of trying to come up with innovative ways to increase revenues and profits.

In my mid-twenties, I fulfilled a dream of going back to school and earning a law degree. During law school, I was fortunate enough to have the opportunity to clerk in the summers for some of the major law firms in my area. I hadn't intended on becoming a full time lawyer as I still thought of myself as an entrepreneur. However, as a young married man, I decided to venture out to see what it was like to work for someone else. In addition, I was excited to learn that as an associate of the law firm I would get paid twice a month! I was accustomed to getting paid whatever was left in the bank account after everyone else had been paid.

I threw myself into my new profession. As with all first year associates, I was "green" and had much to learn. While I was learning the actual craft of practicing law, I also sought to use my entrepreneurial experience to grow the business of the firm. I was interested in health law, so I become actively involved in forming a health law practice. I enjoyed business development, so I worked hard to form relationships and bring in business. After my first year of practice, I had a rude awakening. In the legal industry, many law firms utilize what is known as a "lock step" system of compensation. Essentially, every lawyer at a certain level in terms of years of practice receives the same base pay increase no matter how great or small his or her contribution. While I knew this system was in place going into my job, in my naiveté I thought that surely there were exceptions!

At the end of my first year of employment, the partner in charge of the associates called a meeting with all of the first year associates to discuss our performance and compensation. The partner thanked us for our service to the firm and announced a small percentage increase for the following year which would apply equally to everyone. My heart sank. I realized that no matter what I did, the only way to advance in the organization was to get a year older and slowly work my way up to be eligible for partnership. While it was a great firm and the compensation structure was more than fair, my motivation was zapped. Being in that type of incentive structure for the next seven to eight years seemed like an eternity. It was then that I realized that, if I was going to be motivated in my work, I needed a structure in place to reward my personal contribution to the team. Within six months, I left the firm to work for a startup technology company with a compensation structure better suited to my needs for financial incentives.

What is an Incentive?

For our purposes, we define an incentive as "something that motivates or encourages someone to perform an action." We live in a world of incentives. Our massively complex tax system is designed to incentivize certain behaviors. For example, tax deductions for mortgage interest are designed to encourage home ownership. Corporations offer reward programs to incentivize us for customer loyalty and repeat business. In an employer-employee context, we think of incentives primarily related to compensation. These are usually in the form of bonus plans, stock options, or other commission models.

Let's Make a Deal

In the marketplace, we trade our time, talent, and energy for money. In an organization, this trade takes place between the employer and the employee. The employer seeks to accomplish its goals and objectives. In order to do that, it needs its employees to perform certain actions. These actions are the job functions that are assigned to the employee. Therefore, much time and effort is usually spent on creating financial compensation that adequately incentivizes employees to perform those functions.

While financial incentives are certainly important, they alone don't get the job done of incentivizing employees. What truly incentivizes employees is to feel valued and appreciated.

Drs. Gary Chapman and Paul White in their book *The Five Languages of Appreciation in the Workplace* make a strong case for the importance of organizations showing authentic appreciation to employees. They point out that one of the key mistakes that employers make is to treat everyone as if they receive appreciation the same way. They explain how people actually have a unique "language" in which they tend to share and receive appreciation. These languages are *words of affirmation, quality time, acts of service, tangible gifts*, and *physical touch*. Unfortunately, employers spend millions of dollars annually on recognition programs that fail to truly take into account people's individual needs and "language."

Nobody likes to make a poor deal. I (Martin) bought a car a few years ago that was supposed to be one of the most reliable cars on the market. After thoroughly researching the topic, I traded my money for an automobile that I hoped would provide me reliable transportation for years to come. Unfortunately, about one year after purchasing the vehicle, problems started to occur. Over the next six months, I spent countless hours at the dealership as the mechanics made unsuccessful attempts to fix the car. I grew increasingly frustrated as I believed I'd made a poor deal. What I'd hoped would be a great car turned out to be a lemon.

Unfortunately, in a work context poor deals are struck every day. We believe that it's critical for employers and employees to better consider the bargain to create a win-win arrangement. The normal process is to hire someone and assign them job functions. In exchange, the employee is paid a wage for his or her services. As the research cited above demonstrates, compensation is only one element of this bargain. What organizations need are not just "clock punchers" who provide just enough effort not to be fired. Instead, they need people who give their discretionary effort and contribute to achieving the mission and goals of the organization. Managers are on the front lines of creating a more productive work environment for their employees. To do this, they have to recognize how to better meet the needs of the individual members of their teams. For employees, it's important to increase their self-awareness of what truly incentivizes their top performance.

The Hierarchy of Needs

We should stop and consider psychologist's Abraham Maslow's well known hierarchy of needs pyramid.

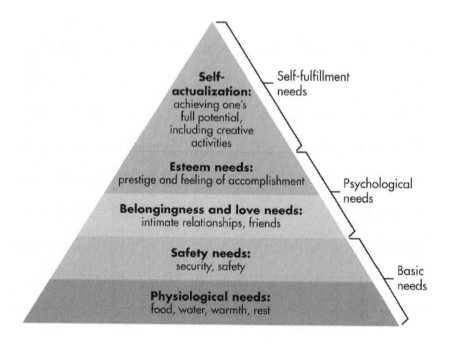

Compensation allows employees to address the fundamental need for safety and address basic physiological needs. Money allows us to put food on the table, a roof over our heads, and clothes on our backs. However, as we look at the pyramid, we also see that as human beings we have a need for appreciation and the need to belong. These needs are not simply met with a paycheck. We find that if a person's needs in these areas are not being met in the workplace, then as soon as they are able they will typically seek employment that fulfills those needs.

Unfortunately, often both employer and employee aren't truly aware of the deeper needs that drive behavior. We encourage people to have greater self-awareness and organizational awareness. This allows employers and employees to create a more impactful and productive relationship. As a legacy of the industrial age mindset, it's easy for employers to treat employees as easily replaceable. Instead, employees are individuals with hopes, dreams, aspirations, and needs. If they believe in the mission of the organization, and are getting their needs met, they will be more engaged and productive. We like to remind our clients that *Productive People Produce Profits. Period!*

Mass Customization

The recipe for success with incentives is "mass customization." We recognize that employers have to be able to scale their incentive programs and address the needs of hundreds, if not thousands, of employees. There must be standards and procedures in place. However, a focus on creating a level of customization as a part of these processes will pay large dividends to the employer. Instead of a "one size fits all" program, an employer can create programs that recognize the needs of individuals.

Rochester, New York based Brand Integrity™ created a solution to help employers incentivize employees through greater individual recognition and appreciation. By utilizing Brand Integrity's Potential Point™ software, award-winning companies such as Wegmans Foods are routinely acknowledging and celebrating employee behaviors that are consistent with the company's core values. These celebrations take the form of posts on an intra-firm social media site that allows employee performance to be recognized and commented on by fellow employees. This type of positive behavior reinforcement results in higher employee engagement and more satisfied customers. Employee appreciation pro-grams like this are very different from the standard recognition pro-grams that simply celebrate employee tenure. In fact, 87% of the annual $46 billion that employers spend on recognition programs is typically spent on tenure (length of service) programs versus performance-based. Unfortunately, there's little evidence that tenure programs actually im-pact corporate performance.

Consider What Incentivizes You

To assist you in thinking through what incentivizes you, we've summa-rized some of the key considerations below:

Public vs. Private
You'll note contrasting preferences of whether you like to address com-pensation as part of a group or whether you consider it a private matter. In the example we gave at the beginning of the chapter, the compensa-tion was addressed as a group and had no customization.

Security vs. Risk
Are you more motivated by a steady paycheck or would you prefer to have less guaranteed compensation and a greater potential income (e.g. commission)? In the example that Martin shared, he was more moti-vated by performance when he had the opportunity to excel and his compensation was at risk.

Tangible vs. Intangible
As we discussed above, incentives are not just about tangible compensa-tion. To what degree are you motivated by intangibles such as variety in your work or greater control over your schedule? For example, in his book, *Drive*, Daniel Pink explained that studies have shown that what really motivates most people in the workplace is the ability to have au-tonomy in their work, the ability to have mastery in continuing to meet new challenges, and to have a sense of purpose in their work. Consider your current job and what intangibles may be present or lacking.

Reflection

1. What three actions, events, or rewards incentivize you?

2. What three actions, events, or rewards disincentivize you?

3. What incentivizes you to go to work each day?

"So, more than anything else in your life, perhaps, it is very, very important to know what motivates you and to make sure that there is not too big a gap between this and what you do with your life."

—IAN ROBERTSON, PH.D.

CHAPTER 7:
MOTIVATING ME FOR BEST PERFORMANCE

Dan Buettner in his bestseller *The Blue Zones* recounts the efforts of his team to "reverse engineer" the secrets of longevity in certain communities. They identified and studied five communities around the globe that had the highest life expectancy or the highest proportions of people who reached age one hundred. After studying these groups, Buettner was able to distill nine characteristics of these groups which he calls the Power 9®. Interestingly, one of those nine is that these people understood their purpose. One of the groups, the Okinawans in Japan, called it "Ikigai" and the Nicoyans from Costa Rica call it "plan de vida." Both of these phrases equate to "Why I wake up in the morning." In fact, Buettner concluded that "Knowing your sense of purpose is worth up to seven years of extra life expectancy."

We spend a great deal of our life at work. In fact, the average American will spend approximately 91,250 hours at work during a lifetime. If we stop and think about that for a moment, we realize that is an incredible amount of time, particularly if we lack a sense of purpose and motivation for our work. What a tragedy to go through a lifetime and never tap into that greater purpose for your life. Henry David Thoreau captured this in his famous quote, "Most men lead lives of quiet desperation and go to the grave with the song still in them."

We believe this should not be the case. However, it takes intentionality to "swim against the current" of life and to choose your own path. Too often, we get stuck living someone else's vision for our life instead of our own.

Understanding Our Needs

As referenced earlier in the book, Abraham Maslow created his "Theory of Needs" in the 1940s. In his theory, he identified the basic needs that we have as human beings: physiological needs, safety needs, and the needs for belonging, self-esteem, and self-actualization. Psychologist David McClelland built upon this foundation in the 1960s by identifying three motivators that we all have. McClelland believed that these motivators are learned and apply regardless of our gender, culture, or age. His theory was that one of these three motivators will be our dominant motivating driver. The three motivators are achievement, affiliation, and power. These motivators are often unconscious but are drivers that shape the course of our personal and working lives.

Here is a summary of McClelland's dominant characteristics.

DOMINANT MOTIVATOR	CHARACTERISTICS OF THIS PERSON'S NEEDS
Achievement	• Has a strong need to set and accomplish challenging goals. • Takes calculated risks to accomplish their goals. • Likes to receive regular feedback on their progress and achievements. • Often likes to work alone.
Affiliation	• Wants to belong to the group. • Wants to be liked, and will often go along with whatever the rest of the group wants to do. • Favors collaboration over competition. • Doesn't like high risk or uncertainty.
Power	• Wants to control and influence others. • Likes to win arguments. • Enjoys competition and winning. • Enjoys status and recognition.

Meeting Your Needs at Work

Frederick Herzberg in his 1968 classic *Harvard Business Review* article "One More Time, How Do You Motivate Employees," asserted that the way to motivate employees was to enrich their jobs. He argued that employees would get more psychological satisfaction and would perform better if they were challenged intellectually. While this certainly applies to many people, it doesn't apply universally. Since then, there have been numerous studies on what motivates employees.

For example, Dr. David Sirota, in his book *The Enthusiastic Employee* shared the results of his extensive research into ways of motivating employees. His team surveyed over four million workers around the world, and he concluded that "the way to enthuse workers is to give them what they want." His "Three-Factor Theory of Human Motivation in the Workplace" is based on three fundamental principles:

- The organization's goals are not in conflict with the workers' goals.
- Workers have basic needs that organizations should try to meet.
- Staff enthusiasm is a source of competitive advantage.

Similarly, author Daniel Pink summarized a great deal of the research on employee motivation in his book *Drive: The Surprising Truth About What Motivates Us.* Pink's own Twitter summary of his book states, "Carrots & Sticks are so last Century. *Drive* says for 21st Century work, we need to upgrade to autonomy, mastery, and purpose." As organizations seek greater performance, they soon realize that getting the most out of their people is the best way to do that. However, this task is easier said than done. It would be easy if we all shared the same needs – but we don't! As individuals, we are complex creatures shaped by our life experiences. A one-size-fits-all approach to managing and motivating us will not work. Instead, you have to take into account our individual differences and needs.

What Motivates You?

We encourage our clients to raise their sense of self-awareness and create systems and processes to encourage communication. Our use of the **UMMD™** Report is one tool that we use to accomplish that objective. In the report, one of the sections is entitled "What Motivates Me for

Best Performance?" When our clients take the assessment, the report generates customized descriptions of what motivates that person. For example, we've shared below the respective report section for both of us:

Carl

- I may respond better to general rather than specialized management tasks.

- I'm motivated by hands-on opportunities.

- I enjoy working with documentation, or documenting processes myself.

- I prefer direct, no-nonsense instructions and encouragement.

- I'm most self-motivated when I'm allowed some time to work alone or with a very small group.

- I'm driven by ideals and principles as much as by concrete incentives.

- I often respond well to ambitious targets and goals.

- Don't force me to make fast decisions.

Martin

- I'm motivated in situations that require a more strategic approach to interacting with People.

- I respond readily to opportunities to influence others directly.

- I'm particularly responsive to situations where I can help others.

- I enjoy working with documentation, or documenting processes myself.

- I like projects which involve the spoken word or which have an auditory component.

- To get the best from me, impose a minimum of rules and procedures.

- I'm considerably self-motivated by incentives directly linked to my performance.

- I'm more self-motivated when I'm permitted to schedule myself.

- I need to feel self-confident about tasks that I may take on if I'm to feel strongly motivated.

- Allow me to be a little unorthodox on occasion.

- Don't force me to make fast decisions.

In our reports, you will see some similarities but also some differences. As we worked together on this book, it was important for us to consider both our similarities and differences to make sure our needs were being met. Again, if our needs aren't being met then we won't bring our best performance to the task at hand. We may in the short term, but it's hard to sustain that for the long term.

Purpose and Motivation

We regularly help individuals and organizations clarify their purpose. By doing this, we help them keep the main thing, the main thing. It's usually a process of discovery. We work with our clients to help them separate the great from the good in their lives. We ask challenging questions and help people to consider what's truly important. Through this process, our clients strip away the nonessentials and grasp their "Why"—their purpose. Motivation is closely related to this. As noted above, we have different things that motivate us and create an optimum work environment. These are based on deeply felt needs.

For example, both of us share a strong resolve to help optimize individual, team, and organizational performance. It's our mission, our passion. It's our "plan de vida," our reason to wake up in the morning. As described above, our motivations are slightly different. Our own life experiences shape our deep motivations for doing what we do.

In my (Martin) life, I've gone through a process of learning what really motivates me. Having lived through financial hardship when my family business went under when I was in high school, I became very focused as I began my career on seeking money and financial security. I still had dreams and ambitions, but they lay dormant while I chased these ambitions. As I was getting older, I had several family members who died young, and I started to question this "deferred life" program I was on. It no longer became acceptable to wait until "someday" to live the life of mission and purpose I craved in my heart. I've made many mistakes along this journey, but I've tried my best to get off of the deferred life program. Unfortunately, the deferred life program is alive and well in our society. Apple founder Steve Jobs wisely noted in a speech at Stanford that "Death is very likely the single best invention of life. It is life's change agent." He went on to remind the students that "Your time is limited, so don't waste it living someone else's life."

As I began to rethink my purpose, I realized that I was highly motivated by a desire to make a difference in people's lives. I began to understand that I really valued autonomy and wanted to be able to set my own schedule. I learned that I really enjoy communicating with people and would rather interact with people than my computer. I began to make changes in my life. Not overnight, but over a gradual period of time, I better aligned my day to day work life with my motivations.

As a business lawyer by training and practice, I decided to open my own law firm to give me greater autonomy over my work and clients. This was a positive step in my journey, but I wasn't quite there. After several years, I realized that my desire to equip and inspire others to meet their full potential wasn't being met as a business lawyer. While

I was incorporating these ideas into my legal practice with my clients, I wasn't fully immersed in helping people, teams, and organizations be their very best. I knew a change needed to occur.

With patient encouragement from Carl, I began to morph my legal practice into a coaching and consulting practice. It took time to make this change—probably longer than it should have because of my fears and insecurities. I then decided to complete this transition by merging my law practice into another firm and taking a position with a coaching and consulting company. As I made this transition, I realized that I'd made a big but important decision to align my daily work around my deepest needs and motivations. I was better positioned to live out my own purpose in life.

Similarly, one of our clients, Geoff, was struggling with a work situation where he was losing his motivation. His business partner was older and expected Geoff to keep the same hours and schedule he did. His partner was an empty nester and workaholic, but Geoff had two young kids at home. Geoff struggled with the relationship; he was conflicted about the long hours and his desire to be a good husband and father. Through the coaching process, Geoff became much more aware of his own motivations and desire to have more flexibility and freedom in his workday. He realized that because his needs weren't being met he was exhibiting stress behaviors both at home and work.

As he learned to better understand himself, he also took time to better understand the motivations of his partner. Though awkward at first, they began to talk. They discussed their preferred work styles and needs. Geoff reorganized his schedule and was able to work more from his home office and spend more time with his family. He and his partner worked out a schedule to make sure they met regularly to address important business decisions. Through this process, they went from being on the verge of splitting up their partnership to finding a way to create a high performance organization that allowed each of them to meet their needs.

Conclusion

You know you better than anyone else. However, many things may lie below the conscious level, so it takes some digging to understand your deeper needs and motivators. This journey of discovery is critical to complete. It will empower you to make better decisions about your life at home and at work. You'll be able to work better in teams because you won't fall into unproductive habits and patterns of behavior because of your needs not being met. You'll live as a more authentic person with transparency and purpose. We encourage you to begin the journey!

"Know yourself to improve yourself."

–AUGUST COMTE

Reflection

1. What gets you excited?

2. What propels you toward you goals?

3. What does being motivated mean to you?

*"The greatest good you can do for another is not just
share your riches, but to reveal to him, his own."*

— BENJAMIN DISRAELI

CHAPTER 8:

WHY SHOULD I HELP OTHERS BE THEIR BEST?

In this book, we've talked a great deal about raising your own level of self-awareness. We've encouraged you look inward and understand what truly motivates you. In this process, we hope that you're gaining clarity and the ability to help your colleagues to understand how to best communicate and work with you. As a result of being intentional about sharing with others how best to work with you, you'll be more productive, reduce conflict, and have better relationships at work. In this chapter, we'll shift the focus and think about the importance of helping others elevate by understanding their motivational drivers.

I (Martin) start with a very personal example. I've shared some in this book about my journey from being a business attorney to a strategic consultant. I'd known for several years that I wanted to make this transition, but I was stuck. I couldn't seem to make the switch and clung to my law career like a child holds on to a favorite blanket. I wouldn't let it go. Two people helped me better understand my motivations, clarify my path, and make this next step in my career. One was my co-author Carl. Carl helped me gain a much deeper understanding of myself. Through his example and encouragement, I realized that I could make this transition. He coached and encouraged me along the way. For that, I'm forever grateful.

I was also encouraged by my friend and colleague Andy Wimberly. Andy had made a successful transition from being a financial advisor to being an executive coach. As he says, "It took me fifteen years to become an overnight success as a coach," but his example and encouragement reinforced my confidence. Both Andy and Carl reached out and helped me help myself. They challenged me and created accountability. They wouldn't let me just "talk the talk" about change; I had to "walk the walk." They shared and continue to share their wisdom and life experiences with me. I use the examples of Carl and Andy to illustrate the point that there's a significant impact to helping others be their best.

I use these personal examples because I want to emphasize the positive impact on the individual who is being helped. If you are the one investing in the life of someone else there are tremendous rewards as well. Since others have invested in me (Martin), I have a sense of duty to pass it on to others. Following the lead of my mentors, I've purposefully invested myself in others. There's a great satisfaction that comes from watching people develop and grow. It's with great pride that I watch leaders I've mentored go on to accomplish their dreams and goals.

Achievements Are Made With and Through People

Herbert Hoover, the United States' 31st President, emphasized our country's "rugged individualism." He believed that the U.S. faced a decision between "the American system of 'rugged individualism' or the choice of a European system of diametrically opposed doctrines— doctrines of paternalism and state socialism. The acceptance of these ideas meant the destruction of self-government through centralization of government; it meant the undermining of initiative and enterprise upon which our people have grown to unparalleled greatness."

Regardless of your political views on this point, there's no denying that the emphasis on individualism and a "frontier mentality" runs deep in our culture. These concepts are related to the "American Dream"— the idea that each of us can have upward mobility through hard work.

These ideas go all the way back to the Declaration of Independence and the belief that "all men are created equal" and that each of us has an inalienable right to "life, liberty, and the pursuit of happiness." James Truslow Adams coined the term "American Dream" in his 1931 book *Epic of America.* He stated, "The American Dream is that dream of a land in which life should be better and richer and fuller for every man, with opportunity for each according to ability or achievement." Horatio Alger famously captured the spirit of this ethos in his novels encouraging young people with his "rags to riches" stories. To this day, the Horatio Alger Association has an annual award for "outstanding individuals in society who have succeeded in the face of adversity."

We emphasize these cultural patterns because it's easy to take them for granted and not realize the impact on our thinking and our lives. While there are many very positive aspects to these ideas, we can sometimes fail to understand the limitations. We can't lose sight of the idea that the greatest successes in life are made with and through people. Great achievements in life are never solo endeavors. Sometimes we forget that. We can be like the turtle on the fencepost. As the story goes, when you find a turtle on top of a fencepost "you know he didn't get there by himself, he doesn't belong there, he doesn't know what to do while he's up there, and just wants someone to help get him down."

In contrast, we can recognize that our success in life comes from the help of others. There's a great expression that we're standing on the shoulders of giants. This quote was first attributed to 12th Century scholar Bernard of Chartres, who used to say, "We are like dwarfs on the shoulders of giants, so that we can see more than them, and things at a greater distance, not by virtue of any sharpness of sight on our part, or any physical distinction, but because we are carried high and raised up by their giant size."

The late Zig Ziglar had a wonderful quote he often repeated: "If you help enough people get what they want in life, you will get what you want." This wasn't a manipulative idea; instead, it's one that recognizes that, by serving others, we truly are helping ourselves.

I (Martin) have been a Rotarian for a number of years. Rotary International (formerly Rotary Club) was formed in 1905 by Paul Harris and three colleagues in Chicago, Illinois. Today, the organization is global, with 1.2 million members, and has addressed some of the world's greatest challenges including the eradication of polio. The Rotary motto of "Service above Self" captures this spirit of service to others. Their previous motto similarly stated: "One profits most who serves best."

When we can walk in humility and realize that our success in life isn't just the result of our own hard work, but due to the help of many others along the way, then we're on our way to being a true leader.

Derrick Rose grew up in Chicago and was a national recruit out of high school as a point guard after winning two state high school championships. He played one season with the University of Memphis where they reached the NCAA championship game. Rose left after his first season and was selected 1st in the 2008 NBA draft by the Chicago Bulls. In his first year as a pro, Rose was selected as "Rookie of the Year." In his second year, he was named an NBA All Star, and in 2011 he was named NBA Most Valuable Player for the league, which made him the youngest player to receive that honor.

In his acceptance speech, Rose looked uncomfortable in the face of the accolades, and he thanked at length all of the individuals who had helped him along the way. He recognized that his success was based on all of the contributions that these people had made to his life. He thanked basketball greats and Chicago Bulls legends Michael Jordan and Scottie Pippen for laying the foundation for the team's success. And he thanked his mother, Brenda Rose, saying about her: "She is my heart, the reason I play the way I play, just everything. Just knowing the days I don't feel right, going to practice, having a hard time, I think about her when she had to wake me up, go to work and make sure I was all right.... You kept me going. I love you and appreciate you being in my life."

Rose's humility and recognition of the contribution of others to his success is rare in today's celebrity culture. One reporter noted, "Rose is quick to deny himself and in turn exalt others. His humility is wondrously refreshing and quite frankly, an anomaly. In a sports culture where narcissism is customary, Rose exudes a counter-cultural, meek posture." Rose, and others with his attitude, realize they don't achieve success by themselves. They are gracious and recognize the value of others in the journey of life.

Building a Great Team

Once we recognize that success in life is not a solo act, we can begin to consider the importance of building up others to create a great team. An organization with high performance teams will go further, faster. Teams are built on a foundation of trust. One of the ways to build trust is to invest yourself in the lives of others. What does this mean? It means that you help other people elevate and achieve their goals and objectives. Unfortunately, this is rare. We're typically so caught up in the tyranny of the urgency of our own matters that we don't stop and consider the hopes, dreams, and aspirations of others. Think about it—do you really know what your colleagues are seeking out of life? Do you know what motivates them to get out of bed in the morning? What would be the difference if you did?

By taking the time to understand your colleagues' motivational drivers you're investing yourself in their lives. We'll talk at length in the next chapter about how you go about doing this, but here we want to emphasize that you have to ask questions and open the lines of communication. Think about the Ziglar quote we referenced above. How are you going to help others get what they want in life if you don't even know what that is? Too often we *assume* we know these things. However, we know what can happen when we *assume* incorrectly.

Building a great team is a challenge. Especially those teams that are thrown together to accomplish difficult tasks. You may have people with different backgrounds, personalities, and communication styles. How do you quickly align yourself and move positively toward stated objectives? Rather than relying solely on hunches or intuition to figure out how to work together, take the time on the front end to consider these differences and to be intentional about learning each other's preferred styles. As we've emphasized, don't just treat people the way you want to be treated, treat them the way *they* want to be treated. It takes time to develop a high performance team, but we truly believe you can accelerate this process through better front end communication and investing in each other.

The Rewards

There are both intrinsic and extrinsic rewards for investing yourself in helping people to be their best. We find that when you help others be their best that you feel better about yourself. I (Martin) write a weekly column on leadership. I've interviewed hundreds of leaders for this column and one of the standard questions I ask is, "What is your proudest moment as a leader?" By far, the most frequent response I'm given is the satisfaction that comes from seeing others develop and move on to achieving great things. There's typically no direct financial reward for these leaders for that kind of success. However, by watching others they invested in succeed, they were able to see how their investment paid off. They could see the fruit of their efforts.

While we're (the authors) separated by a generation, we're both at the age where we've seen people that we've invested in go on to do great things. We share in that intrinsic satisfaction of seeing others elevate themselves. That's one of the main reasons we chose our line of work—we enjoy seeing others be their very best. Perhaps Ralph Waldo Emerson said it best when noted, "The purpose of life is not to be happy. It is to be useful, to be honorable, to be compassionate, to have it make some difference that you have lived and lived well."

There are also extrinsic rewards of investing in others. You'll clearly be a more effective leader if you build up others. Your teams and organization will prosper when there's the trust and respect that comes from a culture of service. Your boss will note if you're a balcony person who lifts people up or a basement person who brings people down. In his bestselling book *Good to Great*, Jim Collins describes his findings that the most successful leaders were what he called "Level 5" leaders who had a rare combination of humility and determination. However, we don't believe that our own advancement should be the goal—it's simply a byproduct. If you can develop a genuine and authentic desire to help others be their best, you'll end up being on the fast track to success as a result.

In the next chapter, we'll explain how you develop and implement strategies to help people be their best. As we close this chapter, we've provided a few questions to reflect on.

Reflection

1. Who has invested in your life?

2. What contributions have they made to your success?

3. Have you thanked them for their contribution?

4. Have you "paid it forward" by investing in the lives of others?

5. What would be the difference in your life if you starting helping others be their very best?

"You feel alive to the degree that you feel you can help others."

—JOHN TRAVOLTA

CHAPTER 9:

HOW DO I HELP OTHERS BE THEIR BEST?

I (Carl) recently facilitated a series of discussions between a district manager and each of his twelve employees. Each session followed the same format. First, the employee shared with the manager his/her lifestyle and livelihood goals and the three initiatives they were going to pursue over the next ninety days. From time to time I prompted the employee to describe or explain how the pursuit of a particular Livelihood Goal was going to enable the realization of a Lifestyle Goal. The purpose was to help the employee embed in his/her mindset the importance of his/her actions.

Secondly, the district manager at my prompting asked each employee the following questions: *What am I doing to help make you successful that you wish I would stop doing? What am I not doing to help make you successful that you wish I would start doing?* The manager took copious notes on the responses.

Near the conclusion of each session I asked both the employee and the district manager to tell me what they'd learned from this activity. As you can imagine, the responses were wide and varied. One recently hired but experienced employee said that, as a result of this experience, she'd come to realize that this was the first time in her work career that a manager had ever helped her connect what she did for a living with what she wanted out of life. Furthermore, she said that being able to provide feedback to the manager on ways he could help her be more successful made her feel even better about her decision to join the organization.

Later, the district manager obtained a large white board and wrote the following question at the top of the board: *Have I earned the right to lead?* Then, beside each of his employees' names he wrote a brief statement committing to do what they'd either asked him to do or not to do to help make them successful. He told his employees that this was going to be his focus for the next ninety days. His commitment was visible, specific, and heartfelt. This white board was going to serve as his information center, or managerial dashboard, to keep him focused on the real reason he was there—to bring out the best in each person!

Our days can be filled with interactions with various mechanical and electronic devices that can also serve as informational centers or dashboards. When I (Carl) open my refrigerator door the information panel on the door tells me the temperature in the refrigerator, in the freezer, and whether or not the air and water filters are in need of replacement. The information center is smart enough to let me know when I should order replacement filters and provides enough time for their arrival. It then lets me know when to replace the filters.

As I drive to work, my SUV dashboard is full of helpful gauges and dials. This morning, for instance, it informed me that I had a half a tank of fuel, that I needed to add windshield washer fluid, that the temperature was 31 degrees, and the snow warning light was glowing red. Arriving at the office, my Mac computer informs me that the batteries are low in my wireless keyboard. My desk clock displays the time, date, and day as well as the room's temperature.

Each of these automatically provided pieces of information are available to help me make better decisions, to think about various options open to me, and to get on with my life and work. Wouldn't it be nice if all of the people we interacted with provided us with crisp, clear, and correct bits of information about their current state of motivation? What do they need today to perform at their optimum level? What do they need from me to be their best? How do they prefer to work today—alone or in teams? What communication exchanges mean the most to them? Are there activities or comments that I should avoid today? What type of incentive is most important to them today? What type of motivational environment is best for them?

Of course, we utilize the *UMMD*™ self-assessment to ascertain each person's responses. We realize that not every reader will have had the opportunity to take the self-assessment or to share and discuss their various preferences. Our recommended solution is that you consider using a series of powerful questions that discover a person's important preferences. Simply ask a person and then listen deeply.

Using Powerful Discovery Questions

Recently, while meeting with a client and one of his employees about the employee's Lifestyle and Livelihood Goals for the current quarter, I (Carl) facilitated a discussion between the two individuals to help them better understand each other and how best to help each other unleash their greatness. Neither had taken the *UMMD*™ self-assessment. Below are the questions I used. Dan is the manager. Cecil is the employee.

Topic: Cecil's Work Preferences

"How does Dan help support your preferred approach to how you do your work?
"Is there anything you wish Dan would start doing to help you perform your work?"

Topic: Cecil's Communication Preferences

"What is it about how Dan talks with you that you really appreciate?"
"Is there anything in the way Dan talks with you that you wish he would modify somewhat?"

Topic: Biggest Mistakes Dan Can Make with Cecil

"Is there anything Dan does when interacting with you that makes you feel uncomfortable in any way?"

Topic: What Incentivizes Cecil?

"Can you share with Dan what incentivizes you?"
"What type of interactions act as a disincentive for you?"

Topic: The Best Way to Motivate Cecil

"In your everyday life and in your work, what three conditions must be present for you to feel really good about yourself and what you do?

With these questions alone, the discussion lasted nearly forty-five minutes. Both Dan and Cecil thought their discussion was beneficial. They agreed to continue their fact-finding discussion and to take the **UMMD™** self-assessment to provide more detailed, in-depth coverage of the five topics. This fact-finding approach doesn't replace taking the **UMMD™** self-assessment. However, these or similar insightful questions can be useful in helping others become their best. Any time spent thinking about and discussing ways to improve interaction between two people is time well invested.

Discovery Questions

Many of my (Carl's) capability coaching sessions are via telephone. The client is responsible for preparing the discussion agenda and taking the lead in her/his growth journey. In these situations we both have exchanged our **UMMD™** Reports and have developed an appreciation for the optimum way to interact with each other. Sometimes, however, I have the opportunity to have a discussion with a potential client or an individual who's interested in knowing more about what to expect from a capability coaching experience. In these cases, neither of us have the benefit of a **UMMD™** Report.

Here are some discovery questions that I have found useful.

General

1. What went well for you last year, both in your life and in your career that you'd like to repeat this coming year?

2. Was there anything you did last year that didn't work out quite as well as you expected?

3. Is there anything you'd like to tweak or do differently this next year to bring you closer to your desired lifestyle?

Lifestyle Goals

1. How do you want to be remembered by your family and friends?

2. If you knew you were going to die in three years how would you live your life?

3. What would you attempt to do if you knew you couldn't fail?

Motivational Drivers

1. When you're at your best, what are you best at doing or being? Why?

2. To what extent are you engaged in activities or goals that you are passionate about?

3. To what extent are you fully using your strengths, abilities, and skills?

4. To what extent are you in an environment where you're being treated by others like you want to be treated?

Active Listening

Asking powerful discovery questions is only one part of the process to improve understanding between two people. Active listening is another part. Listening to what is said, what isn't said, what is felt, and what is meant requires concentration. One must be fully engaged in the active listening process. You can't be thinking about what you'll say or ask the person next. You can't let your mind wander to make judgments. You want to be fully present in the moment. Without active listening, it will be impossible to effectively act on what the other person is sharing and discussing with you.

Listen for the general trend of the discussion. Is the person using questions such as "How can I...?" or "What can I do...?" These might indicate a sense of personal accountability. Or, are they using questions such as "When are you going...?" Or, "Why can't you...?" which might indicate an avoidance of personal accountability. For a more detailed treatment of the personal accountability topic refer to John G. Miller's book *QBQ! The Question Behind The Question*. Here are some comparison questions Miller uses to make his point.

AVOIDING ACCOUNTABILITY	EMBRACING ACCOUNTABILITY
Why do we have to go through all this change?	How can I adapt to the changing world?
Who dropped the ball?	How can I contribute?
When is somebody going to train me?	What can I do to develop myself?
When is that department going to do its job right?	What can I do to solve the problem?

Observing Facial and Gestural Behaviors

As discussed earlier in this book, in face-to-face communication exchanges, a person's nonverbal behavior more accurately conveys the person's feeling about the topic being discussed. Does the person's general posture suggest their mindset is open or closed? Does the person appear relaxed, nervous, or distracted? How about eye contact? Gestures? Like words, one's nonverbal gestures can have various meanings, especially in different cultural settings, so caution is advised. How aligned does the person's nonverbal behavior appear to be with the actual words spoken and tone of voice? Inconsistencies might be an indication that you should listen more intently and/or ask a nonthreatening open-ended question or two.

Group Situations

I (Carl) am often invited to sit in and observe meetings of management teams. Usually, I don't have a speaking role. I'm just there to gain valuable background information about the organization and some of its opportunities or challenges.

Here are some behaviors I look for:

- Is there an understanding about why the topic is being discussed?

- What is the purpose of the discussion? Is it information sharing, problem analysis, problem solving, assignment of blame, excuse embracing, delaying action, or determining action steps to be taken?

- Who is acting as a clarifier when the discussion gets fuzzy?

- Is someone accepting the role of a mediator?

- Is there a summarizer?

- Who is keeping the meeting on track? Who is managing the time?

- Who is dominating the discussion?

- Who seeks the opinions of those who might be more reserved?

- Who introduces solutions? And, how?

- Who demonstrates possibility thinking? Creative thinking?

- Who likes to state reasons why things can't be done?

- How effective is the leader of the meeting? Is it clear who the leader is?

- To what extent is there a commitment to follow up or follow-through?

- What confirming or conflicting messages are being communicated by body language?

- How relaxed does the group appear?

- What unspoken tensions seem to be present?

- Are certain individuals being systematically excluded from the discussion?

Reflection

1. Is there someone in your life who's bringing out the best in you?

2. How do you bring out the best in others?

3. How do you bring out the best in yourself?

"Awareness without action is worthless."

— PHIL MCGRAW

CHAPTER 10:
CALL TO ACTION

Life is too short and time too precious to spend our lives performing tasks that do not create growth or are not personally rewarding. One of the greatest educational experiences I (Carl) had was a job as an unskilled laborer loading and unloading forty-foot trailers during the summer while in college. The working conditions were hot, sometime risky, and always physically challenging. I was grateful for the opportunity to have this work and the pay was quite good. In fact, I was able to save enough money in twelve weeks to support myself for the rest of the year. I did this type of work for three summers. I was blessed.

The greatest revelation, however, was the realization that I was performing work that was not in alignment with my major interest—namely working with people rather than things. While I was always treated with respect by management and my co-workers, the reality of the situation was that there were no growth opportunities, no variety in duties, and no chance of being creative. In short, several of my major motivational drivers weren't being fulfilled. I was indeed blessed. Blessed in the sense that, despite the great pay and the opportunity to finance my college education in full, I knew that just working for money would leave a "hole in my soul."

I, of course, wanted more. I wanted an opportunity to make a difference, not just in what I did for a living, but in my interactions with others in the world. For more than thirty-six years I've had the opportunity to work with great people in great organizations in a variety of industries throughout the United States. As an active executive coach and management consultant I've learned a great deal about people and about organizations.

One undeniable conclusion I've reached is that great individuals make the organization great—individuals who are actively engaged in their work, doing what they love to do, doing what they do best, and being treated by others as they want to be treated. Martin and I want to help you, the reader, be great. We want you to be all that you're capable of being. We want to help you bring out the best in yourself and the best in others. That is how you unlock the growth potential of your organization!

Reflection

1. What would you attempt to do if you knew you could not fail?

2. Three years hence what would have had to happen in your life for you to feel positive about the steps you took today?

Call to Action

We want you to experience the sense of satisfaction you receive from confirming and sharing your motivational drivers with another. We want you to unleash your greatness upon the world and make it a better place. By using the coupon code below you can procure your own personalized *UMMD*™ Report for just $49.00—a savings of $50.00 off the retail price of $99.00. Coupon Code **M8M58PDJFP**. Are you willing to invest $49.00 in your future?

The *UMMD*™ Report provides a great framework for two people to enhance their understanding of five important interpersonal dimensions, namely:

> How to work with me
> How to talk with me
> Biggest mistakes you can make with me
> How to incentivize me
> Motivating me for best performance

This report is compiled from your answers to three distinct questionnaires that can be taken online. It takes less than 45 minutes to complete the three questionnaires. More information can be found at www. MyMotivationalDrivers.com. Once on the site, type in your email address, enter the coupon code **M8M58PDJFP**, and hit "apply." The price will adjust to $49.00. Enter your name and payment information and hit "submit." You'll receive an email with a link to take the questionnaires online. Once completed, your personalized *UMMD*™ Report will be emailed directly to you.

Reading and sharing your *UMMD*™ Report could be life changing. Are you ready for your new life?

HOW TO EFFECTIVELY USE THE RESULTS OF THE *UMMD*™ REPORT

How to Effectively Use the Results of Your *UMMD™* Report

The essential fact to remember is that this is a "self-assessment." Each person's report is generated based on his/her responses to a series of choices/statements. Each person gets a personalized report that they can review, confirm, share, and discuss.

The *review and confirm* portion of the process permits a person to check one or two statements for each topic that they deem most significant to them and that they would like to share with others. Once the significant items are identified the report can be emailed or hand delivered to the individual(s) prior to having your sharing discussion.

The *share and discuss* portion of the process allows an individual to communicate with others the best way to interact with them. Here are some guidelines that you might find helpful for this stage of the process.

- First, thank the other individual for taking the time to meet with you.

- Second, explain that the purpose of the motivational drivers report is to increase awareness of the optimum ways to interact with you.

- Ask if there are any questions before you start sharing your most significant motivational drivers.

- Select a topic and read off one of the items you selected as significant and discuss how that item helps bring out the best in you.

- Ask the other person to share his/her thoughts about what you shared.

- It's not necessary to cover all topics in your first meeting. Just get the process started.

- If both parties have **UMMD™** reports, we've found it useful to have both parties share and discuss one topic at a time. For instance, "how to work with me" or "how to talk with me."

- Thank the person again and express how beneficial the discussion has been.

- Put into practice what you learned from this experience.

- Remember the basics, namely: When an individual is being treated like she/he prefers that individual is most likely to be at their best. When they are at their best, they tend to do their best. They are more engaged in their work; more excited about what they do; and more productive in their use of time, effort, and energy.

CARL'S *UNDERSTANDING MY MOTIVATIONAL DRIVERS™* REPORT MARTIN'S *UNDERSTANDING MY MOTIVATIONAL DRIVERS™* REPORT

CARL HICKS

Understanding My Motivational Drivers™

This Growth Group Report contains the following topic(s):

How to work with me
How to talk to me
Biggest mistakes you can make with me
How to incentivize me
Motivating me for best performance

THE
GROWTH GROUP
Consultants to Management
Optimizing individual, team and organizational performance
MyMotivationalDrivers.com
5425 Wisconsin Ave, Suite 600
Chevy Chase, MD 20815
CarlHicks@TheHicksFix.com
(240) 951-4897

Understanding My Motivational Drivers™

Introduction to this Growth Group Report

This report is designed to provide you with an opportunity to let others know how you prefer to be treated. Specifically, this report provides you with a format for sharing with others five very important interpersonal topics:

- How you prefer to work
- Most effective way to talk with you
- Biggest mistakes they should avoid
- How you prefer to be incentivized
- How to motivate you for best performance

Why is it important?

Being your best requires that others treat you as you want to be treated. It is important that your expectations of how you want others to interact with you be understood and appreciated by them. This report can serve as the vehicle that permits you to review, confirm, share and discuss your expectations in an objective manner.

Know Thyself

Each topic in this report contains a number of personal statements generated by your answers to The Birkman® Method questionnaire. Carefully read each statement and check those items that are most significant to you.

Know Me

Share and discuss with others how the statements you checked impact you. You may want to share and discuss this report with a friend, team member, supervisor, colleague, professional associate, business partner, coach, team leader, employee, trusted advisor, client/customer or peer. This proactive step could make a meaningful difference in your life.

1

CARL HICKS: Topic 1: How to work with me

The following personal statements are generated by your answers to The Birkman® Method questionnaire. Carefully read each statement and check the statements that are most significant to you. Discuss with a trusted advisor or friend how your selected statements impact you – past or present

- [ ] Be direct and straightforward with me
- [ ] Don't force group interaction on me constantly
- [ ] Incentivize me using generalized and more abstract rewards
- [ ] Offer me challenging assignments; be aware of my tendency to blame myself for failures
- [ ] Give me plenty of time for complex or difficult decisions

File No. B60414. Presented By Birkman International, Inc. • (713) 623-2760 • info@birkman.com

2

CARL HICKS: Topic 2: How to talk to me

The following personal statements are generated by your answers to The Birkman® Method questionnaire. Carefully read each statement and check the statements that are most significant to you. Discuss with a trusted advisor or friend how your selected statements impact you -- past or present

• [ ] Get to the point. Don't worry too much about hurting my feelings

• [ ] If the subject's important, talk to me alone

• [ ] Emphasize those results which will offer benefits to others as well as me, or which will support my system of personal values

• [ ] Don't downplay any difficulties surrounding the matter we are discussing, and don't flatter me. If the project is extremely demanding, tell me so

• [ ] Don't press me to come to any conclusions in our first encounter. Let the matter settle, and arrange a subsequent conversation with me

File No. B60414. Presented By Birkman International, Inc. • (713) 623-2760 • info@birkman.com

CARL HICKS: Topic 3: Biggest mistakes you can make with me

The following personal statements are generated by your answers to The Birkman® Method questionnaire. Carefully read each statement and check the statements that are most significant to you. Discuss with a trusted advisor or friend how your selected statements impact you -- past or present

- [ ] Beating about the bush with me
- [ ] Forcing me to participate unnecessarily in group activities
- [ ] Forcing me to think and act competitively
- [ ] Telling me that I have done well when that is not really true
- [ ] Pushing me to make up my mind quickly

File No. B60414. Presented By Birkman International, Inc. • (713) 623-2760 • info@birkman.com

4

Consultants to Management

CARL HICKS: Topic 4: How to incentivize me

The following personal statements are generated by your answers to The Birkman® Method questionnaire. Carefully read each statement and check the statements that are most significant to you. Discuss with a trusted advisor or friend how your selected statements impact you -- past or present

- [ ] Talk about remuneration with me privately, not openly
- [ ] Don't overlook the effectiveness of offering me intangible as well as tangible rewards
- [ ] Reward only my attainment of demanding, meaningful achievements

File No. B60414. Presented By Birkman International, Inc. • (713) 623-2760 • info@birkman.com

THE
GROWTH GROUP
Consultants to Management

CARL HICKS: Topic 5: Motivating me for best performance

The following personal statements are generated by your answers to The Birkman® Method questionnaire. Carefully read each statement and check the statements that are most significant to you. Discuss with a trusted advisor or friend how your selected statements impact you -- past or present

- [ ] I may respond better to general rather than specialized management tasks
- [ ] I'm motivated by hands-on opportunities
- [ ] I enjoy working with documentation, or documenting processes myself
- [ ] I prefer direct, no-nonsense instructions and encouragement
- [ ] I'm most self-motivated when I'm allowed some time to work alone or with a very small group
- [ ] I'm driven by ideals and principles as much as by concrete incentive
- [ ] I often respond well to ambitious targets and goals
- [ ] Don't force me to make fast decisions

File No. B60414. Presented By Birkman International, Inc. • (713) 623-2760 • info@birkman.com

6

MARTIN WILLOUGHBY

Understanding My Motivational Drivers™

This Growth Group Report contains the following topic(s):

How to work with me
How to talk to me
Biggest mistakes you can make with me
How to incentivize me
Motivating me for best performance

THE
GROWTH GROUP

Consultants to Management
Optimizing individual, team and organizational performance
MyMotivationalDrivers.com
5425 Wisconsin Ave. Suite 600
Chevy Chase, MD 20815
CarlHicks@TheHicksFix.com
(240) 351-4897

Understanding My Motivational Drivers™

Introduction to this Growth Group Report

This report is designed to provide you with an opportunity to let others know how you prefer to be treated. Specifically, this report provides you with a format for sharing with others five very important interpersonal topics:

- How you prefer to work
- Most effective way to talk with you
- Biggest mistakes they should avoid
- How you prefer to be incentivized
- How to motivate you for best performance

Why is it important?

Being your best requires that others treat you as you want to be treated. It is important that your expectations of how you want others to interact with you be understood and appreciated by them. This report can serve as the vehicle that permits you to review, confirm, share and discuss your expectations in an objective manner.

Know Thyself

Each topic in this report contains a number of personal statements generated by your answers to The Birkman® Method questionnaire. Carefully read each statement and check those items that are most significant to you.

Know Me

Share and discuss with others how the statements you checked impact you. You may want to share and discuss this report with a friend, team member, supervisor, colleague, professional associate, business partner, coach, team leader, employee, trusted advisor, client/customer or peer. This proactive step could make a meaningful difference in your life.

1

MARTIN WILLOUGHBY: Topic 1: How to work with me

The following personal statements are generated by your answers to The Birkman® Method questionnaire. Carefully read each statement and check the statements that are most significant to you. Discuss with a trusted advisor or friend how your selected statements impact you -- past or present

- [ ] Avoid imposing structured plans on me if at all possible
- [ ] Be sure to offer me concrete, material rewards
- [ ] Don't over-schedule me
- [ ] Encourage my natural self-confidence; where possible, offer discreet support if I encounter failure
- [ ] Offer me opportunities to express my individuality
- [ ] Give me plenty of time for complex or difficult decisions

File No. G3GV6S. Presented By Birkman International, Inc. • (713) 623-2760 • info@birkman.com

Consultants to Management

MARTIN WILLOUGHBY: Topic 2: How to talk to me

The following personal statements are generated by your answers to The Birkman® Method questionnaire. Carefully read each statement and check the statements that are most significant to you. Discuss with a trusted advisor or friend how your selected statements impact you -- past or present

• [ ] Where possible, present the big idea to me first and then wait for a response before offering me more detail

• [ ] If there is a financial component to our discussions, emphasize it freely, particularly where I will benefit personally

• [ ] Be prepared to talk the matter over with me in a few short sessions rather than one intensive meeting

• [ ] Try and frame the matter under discussion as something that I can achieve. Show me that you believe I can succeed

• [ ] Encourage me to think "outside the box" if you really want to engage my attention

• [ ] Don't press me to come to any conclusions in our first encounter. Let the matter settle, and arrange a subsequent conversation with me

File No. G3GV6S. Presented By Birkman International, Inc. • (713) 623-2760 • info@birkman.com

3

Consultants to Management

MARTIN WILLOUGHBY: Topic 3: Biggest mistakes you can make with me

The following personal statements are generated by your answers to The Birkman® Method questionnaire. Carefully read each statement and check the statements that are most significant to you. Discuss with a trusted advisor or friend how your selected statements impact you -- past or present

- [ ] Burdening me with unnecessary rules and procedures
- [ ] Failing to follow through on financial commitments made to me
- [ ] Measuring my performance by watching how "busy" I am
- [ ] Criticizing me, particularly in front of others, without mentioning my successes first
- [ ] Making me conform unnecessarily
- [ ] Pushing me to make up my mind quickly

File No. G3GV6S. Presented By Birkman International, Inc. • (713) 623-2760 • info@birkman.com

4

MARTIN WILLOUGHBY: Topic 4: How to incentivize me

The following personal statements are generated by your answers to The Birkman® Method questionnaire. Carefully read each statement and check the statements that are most significant to you. Discuss with a trusted advisor or friend how your selected statements impact you – past or present

- [ ] Make exceptions to structured remuneration plans for me where possible
- [ ] Incentivize me using strictly performance-based criteria. Never retract an incentive-based commitment that you have made to me
- [ ] Focus mainly on what I have achieved or done well when determining remuneration
- [ ] Unorthodox incentives often work well with me

File No. G3GV6S. Presented By Birkman International, Inc. • (713) 623-2760 • info@birkman.com

5

Consultants to Management

MARTIN WILLOUGHBY: Topic 5: Motivating me for best performance

The following personal statements are generated by your answers to The Birkman® Method questionnaire. Carefully read each statement and check the statements that are most significant to you. Discuss with a trusted advisor or friend how your selected statements impact you -- past or present

- [ ] I'm motivated in situations that require a more strategic approach to interacting with people
- [ ] I respond readily to opportunities to influence others directly
- [ ] I'm particularly responsive to situations where I can help others
- [ ] I enjoy working with documentation, or documenting processes myself
- [ ] I like projects which involve the spoken word or which have an auditory component
- [ ] To get the best from me, impose a minimum of rules and procedures
- [ ] I'm considerably self-motivated by incentives directly linked to my performance
- [ ] I'm more self-motivated when I'm permitted to schedule myself
- [ ] I need to feel self-confident about tasks that I may take on if I'm to feel strongly motivated
- [ ] Allow me to be a little unorthodox on occasion
- [ ] Don't force me to make fast decisions

File No. G3GV6S. Presented By Birkman International, Inc. • (713) 623-2760 • info@birkman.com

THE GROWTH GROUP
Consultants to Management

ABOUT THE AUTHORS

Carl F. Hicks, Jr. consults with successful senior executives and business owners who want more. More personal and professional growth. More productivity and profitability. More meaning and happiness. More quality thinking time. More balance between their Lifestyle Goals and their Livelihood Goals. As President/CEO of The Growth Group, LLC, Carl works with some of America's best-managed companies helping them to identify and develop their top managerial talent, strengthen their work teams and optimize their organization's performance. Through his conversational-coaching approach, Carl keeps clients actively engaged and focused on critical strategic initiatives, growth and profitability—while maintaining a balance between their Lifestyle Goals and their Livelihood Goals.

Clients range from emerging entrepreneurs to Fortune 100 firms. His results-oriented approach to management combines a formal management education—Ph.D. in Business Administration and MBA from the University of Arkansas and B.S. in Management with Distinction from Mississippi State University—with more than thirty years of practical consulting experience.

Carl is on the Board of Directors of Lifetime Financial Growth, LLC, serves as a Strategic Advisor for Butler Snow Advisory Services, LLC, and has been recognized by Birkman International as a Senior Birkman Consultant, a designation earned by only 5% of their consultants worldwide. He is the author of *High Impact Ideas For Your Life*, a collection of motivational thoughts and observations designed to inspire you to unleash your greatness.

Martin Willoughby serves as a Principal of Butler Snow Advisory Services. His responsibilities include assisting the CEO in strategic planning and development, managing key relationships, and optimizing the various operations of the firm.

During the past 22 years, Martin has been an equal-parts business consultant, attorney, and entrepreneur with a passion for helping other businesses and individuals accelerate. He has owned and operated successful businesses, strategically advised companies as in-house counsel, and effectively represented clients ranging from individuals to publicly traded entities.

Martin was previously the Managing Member of Willoughby Law Group, PLLC. In this capacity, he served as General Counsel for various well-known software, food, smart grid technology, and pharmaceutical companies. Although Martin is an attorney, he does not provide legal services through Butler Snow Advisory.

Martin also co-founded a facilities management firm (C&W Management), as well as a real estate dot.com (homesquire.com).

Martin is an accomplished public speaker and author, routinely contributing columns to area business and technology publications, including the *Mississippi Business Journal* and *Pointe Innovation.*

His book, ZOOM Entrepreneur (Barringer Publishing, 2011) has received high praise as an orderly playbook on how an entrepreneur should develop a business—from a personality inventory and self-assessment to the execution of a business plan. To learn more, visit www.zoomyourbusiness.com.

ADDITIONAL RESOURCES AVAILABLE FROM THE GROWTH GROUP, LLC

Learn more about our awareness and growth enhancing services.

- **Executive Coaching**
  Expand your scope of possibilities, eliminate perceptual constraints, and journey to your next level of success.

- **Team Strengthening**
  Increase the productivity and profitability of your organization by maximizing your team's effectiveness.

- **Organizational Optimization**
  Align your strategy, structure, staffing, and systems in a way that propels your organization where you want it to go.

Free downloads of:
High Impact Ideas Newsletter
Coaching Tips
White papers
Templates
Publications

For additional information contact:

Carl F. Hicks, Jr., President/CEO
The Growth Group, LLC
5425 Wisconsin Ave, Suite 600
Chevy Chase, MD 20815
240-351-4897
CarlHicks@TheHicksFix.com
www.TheHicksFix.com